"What a fant… fundraising p… assembling this wealth of information in one book. It is invaluable!"

—Birgit Smith Burton, Executive Director of Foundation Relations, Georgia Institute of Technology

"Martin Leifeld has made a generous gift to the world of fundraising: a gem of a book to guide and inspire fundraisers, volunteers, and donors. In *Five Minutes for Fundraising*, Martin has gathered a group of impressive professionals, coaxed them to share their stories, interwoven their nuggets with sound advice, and presented it all in easily digestible segments. Use this as you would a daily devotional. It's that good!"

—Carolyn Grady, Chief Development Officer, YMCA of Greater Pittsburgh

"Practical. Helpful. Easy. Martin Leifeld has put together the best advice in the most user-friendly form. Once read, this book is a reference to be utilized throughout one's development career."

—Mark Conzemius, President of the Catholic Community Foundation for Eastern South Dakota

"Thanks to Martin for sharing his experiences and advice so generously, and for pulling together advice from a variety of colleagues across the profession. We are all running so fast with our day-to-day responsibilities, and Martin's book encourages us to take a moment to remind ourselves of the most important lessons we've learned, and the reasons we got involved in this wonderful profession in the first place."

—Ron Schiller, Founding Partner, Aspen Leadership Group

"Drawing upon Martin Leifeld's deep experience, admirable achievements, and thoughtful reflections, *Five Minutes for Fundraising* is an engaging collection of lessons, guidance, and inspiration certain to lift up any professional fundraiser. But the book is more than the opinions and 'war stories' of one individual (albeit a talented and self-effacing one). It also mines wisdom, expertise, and advice from 26 of today's leading development practitioners, whose insights serve to reinforce and expand upon Martin's informed perspectives."

—Mark W. Jones, J.D., Vice President, Advancement Resources

"Martin has inspired and mentored so many fundraisers throughout his career. This book captures his experiences, shares his knowledge, and offers insights to help current and future fundraisers achieve success."

—Matthew T. White, Vice President, Advancement, and President of the Utah State University Foundation

"Corporate donors want their contributions to align with their corporate mission. In my experience, Martin has done an outstanding job of identifying where the goals of Express Scripts and UMSL intersect as the chief fundraiser for UMSL. Given Martin's proven know-how, this book is a must-read for volunteer fundraisers like myself, professional fundraisers, or someone thinking about volunteering or working for a nonprofit."

**—George Paz, philanthropist,
Chairman of the Board, Express Scripts**

"Martin Leifeld is not only a masterful fundraiser but also a positive motivator and mentor for other fundraisers. In this book, he shares his many 'secrets of success,' including the strong passion he brings to his work, his respect for donors, and his acknowledgment that meaningful and successful fundraising is hard work. In *Five Minutes for Fundraising,* he shares lessons and insights that are certain to enhance the efforts of anyone who seeks to make a difference in this field."

**—Brenda McPhail, retired Associate Vice Chancellor of
University Development, University of Missouri–St. Louis**

"Martin is an expert in major gifts training. He presented an extraordinary program on major gifts recently. Not only did he provide extremely valuable, insightful information on the process of major gift fundraising, he was able to maintain a high level of participant engagement throughout the half-day session. Similarly, Martin's book extends this training to all who read it. Martin is a rock star fundraising trainer!"

—Amy Rome, The Rome Group

"Fundraisers see stories by donors about their interests (often unexpressed until brought forth) as the catalyst for philanthropic engagement. The stories as told here by Leifeld and friends will prompt informed and inspired leadership for even greater 'voluntary action for the public good.'"

—Fred A. Bleeke, Past President,
Lutheran Foundation of Saint Louis

"Martin lives what he teaches. While he is an effective and knowledgeable fundraiser, Martin always puts my interests as a donor and alumnus first and foremost in his interactions with me. He guided me to make a significant philanthropic investment and, in so doing, helped to make the experience a meaningful, memorable one for me."

—Wayne DeVeydt, philanthropist and CEO,
Surgery Partners, Inc.

FIVE MINUTES FOR FUNDRAISING

A Collection of Expert Advice from Gifted Fundraisers

Martin Leifeld

Saint Louis, MO

Five Minutes For Fundraising
A Collection of Expert Advice from Gifted Fundraisers

Copyright © 2018 by Martin Leifeld
All rights reserved. No part of this publication may be reproduced, distributed or transmitted in any form or by any means, including photocopying, recording, or other electronic or mechanical methods, without the prior written permission of the publisher, except in the case of brief quotations embodied in critical reviews and certain other noncommercial uses permitted by copyright law. For permission requests, write to the publisher, addressed "Attention: Permissions Coordinator," at the address below.

ISBN 978-1-7322458-0-8
Library of Congress Control Number: 9781732245808

PO Box 11821
Saint Louis, MO 63105
Printed in the United States

www.MartinLeifeld.com

Author photo: August H. Jennewein
Book design: N-KCreative.com

Ordering Information: Quantity sales or special discounts are available for purchase by corporations, associations, and others. For details, contact FiveMinutesPress@gmail.com.

Dan – thanks you for your friendship, support and wise counsel,

[illegible]

June, 2018

Dedication

For all donors who contribute gifts for worthy causes.
Your gifts matter more than you can know.

For those donors with whom I have been privileged to assist
to make a difference in the lives of others and the world.

For all fundraisers who facilitate gifts of significance.

CONTENTS

ACKNOWLEDGMENTS

This book would not have been possible without the help of many. I especially want to recognize the friends and colleagues whose advice and assistance helped to make this book a reality: Chip Demchak, Katie Harder, Rose Ippolito, Joanne Jarvi, Dan Lauer, Peggy Nehmen, Katherine Pickett, Kathy Thompson, Dick Weiss, Amber Withycombe, and Beth Zdon.

This book was enriched beyond measure by the following group of expert collaborators to whom I owe a debt of gratitude: Mark Berlyn, Fred Bleeke, Birgit Smith Burton, Jeffrey Byrne, Linda Carter, Mark Conzemius, Sergio M. Gonzalez, Carolyn Grady, Jake Heuser, Tom Hiles, Ellen Howe, Larry C. Johnson, Mark W. Jones, Richard K. Jung, Shaun Keister, Orv Kimbrough, Brenda McPhail, Suzy Mink, Joan Nesbitt, Ilene Novack, Felicia Pulliam, Ron Schiller, Carol Schmidt, Matt Senecal, John Sentovich, and Matt White.

It seems that the older I get, the more my family increases in importance. So much of what I have learned about philanthropy began in my earliest years from my parents, the late Matthias and Marian Leifeld. I have five siblings whom I dearly love, all of whom exemplify a philanthropic approach to life: Mary Kay, Beth, Susan, Jeanne, and Chris.

I am richly blessed with four children—Jessica, Rose, John, and Daniel—plus my daughter-in-law, Rubria, and Ben, my son-in-law. And, I have seven grandchildren who fill my heart with joy: Ellie, Piper, Savannah, Cash, Victoria, Josie, and Isabella.

Most of all, I am the most fortunate man on earth to be married to Ellen Howe, who is my rock, my equal partner, and first and foremost in my life.

Thank you for reading this book. I hope it provides you with transformational ideas in your work with donors on behalf of your organization.

INTRODUCTION

I am a fundraiser.

Perhaps you are, too, and hope to get better at what you do. Or maybe you are thinking about becoming a fundraiser and want a quick introduction to the field. You may serve on a board with an expectation to raise funds for the organization. Or perhaps you are frustrated with fundraising and are hoping to find a reason to stick with it. Whatever your reason for picking up *Five Minutes for Fundraising: A Collection of Expert Advice from Gifted Fundraisers,* I am grateful and want to make your reading time worthwhile.

Probably, like many of us, your interest in fundraising is inspired by one or more organizations that you care deeply about. Asking for resources, even if they are not for you, can be uncomfortable. It takes will and courage to ask people for money.

But it is well worth doing. What fundraisers do is ask for money on behalf of outstanding organizations doing important work. We work not only on behalf of these organizations but also on behalf of donors, who want to put their funds to the best possible use. We are, by and large, idealists. Many of us draw motivation, even inspiration, from our causes, which range from spiritual beliefs to being our brother's keeper to repairing the world.

Most of us didn't grow up dreaming about becoming fundraisers. I do know some people who are so successful at this work that you might consider them born fundraisers. But for me it was more nurture, I think, than nature.

It started with my parents. Matt and Marian Leifeld raised my five siblings and me in a small town on the Mississippi River in Minnesota about twenty-five miles south of the Twin Cities. Hastings was home to about five thousand people when I was there (its population has since quadrupled) and my parents were very much a part of the fabric of the community. Dad was a custodian at an elementary school and Mom was what we used to quaintly call a homemaker. They both grew up on farms in the Depression era. The crisis hit my dad's family particularly hard. Neither Mom nor Dad attended high school (though Dad got his commercial boiler license in his fifties and Mom got her GED at age sixty-five). It was their work ethic, intelligence, common sense, deep faith in God, and good intentions that helped them carve out a piece of the American Dream. They cobbled together their savings to buy a home and gave their kids a better life than they enjoyed. They sent us to Catholic grade schools and universities.

Although their resources were limited, Mom and Dad shared what they had. They took in foster children. They attended church faithfully and always tithed from Dad's humble earnings. My mom and dad kept a ledger in pencil listing all our family's expenses. When I would peek from time to time I would see that along with money spent on milk, gas, and other necessities, perhaps $1.25 also went to Guardian Angel's Parish. Did I have any idea how tight things got for my parents? Maybe just an inkling. As the end of the month drew near, Mom would sometimes buy powdered milk to save a few pennies as we awaited Dad's next paycheck.

My parents' generosity was also demonstrated through the way they welcomed friends and family. They invited our elderly relatives in for long stays. This was not always easy, as we lived in an older home where Mom and Dad's bedroom was a converted den and the kids doubled up in the bedrooms.

Then there was the difficult, elderly man, Jim. He had been engaged to my dad's older sister, who tragically died of tuberculosis before they wed. Sadly, he never married. Jim visited regularly but the visits were unsettling. He was an outspoken atheist and prone to using rough language that got under Dad's skin. Once Dad said to Mom, "I'm not sure we should have Jim over anymore." My mom replied that Jim was family and should always be welcome. "You never know," she said, "we might be entertaining an angel."

As it turned out, Jim was a kind of angel. When he died, my parents learned much to their surprise that he had left them his estate, which helped with their debts and eased Dad's passage into retirement.

Even at a young age, I learned from my parents' example in particular ways.

When I was in the fifth grade, a newspaper in the Twin Cities, the *St. Paul Pioneer-Press,* included a nationally syndicated column titled "Ask Andy" that sponsored a competition. Students were invited to ask a question of a science expert, and the child whose question was selected would receive a set of encyclopedias. My teacher, Sister Marie Charles, assigned each student in our class to write a question, all of which would be submitted to the contest. Sister had said that this would be a way for our classroom to gain a set of encyclopedias that we could all share. At least that's how I understood it. That night while doing my homework at the kitchen table I discussed the challenge with my mother and fashioned a question about starfish: "How does a starfish grow back its legs?"

Some weeks later, the phone rang at my home. Sister Marie Charles was on the line. My heart began to race, because I thought for sure that I was in trouble. But not at all. Sister Marie Charles told me the science column had selected my question and we were going to receive the encyclopedias for our home

I was overwhelmed but also nonplussed. Those encyclopedias were supposed to go to the school, not me, I insisted. (It's not that we couldn't have used them; we did not have a complete set of encyclopedias.)

Oh, no, I was assured, the encyclopedias are for you and your family, Martin.

Still, that didn't seem right to me and I stuck to my guns. The encyclopedias were for the school, I insisted, not me. That's why I had submitted my question. When the newspaper leadership heard about my decision, they arranged for executives to come to our school and make an all-school presentation of the encyclopedias to Sister Marie Charles and me. And so, the school graciously accepted those encyclopedias and put a small plaque on the shelf where they sat: "Donated by Martin Leifeld." (I guess I could characterize this as my first major gift.)

A few years later my parents further sacrificed so that I could attend Saint John's Preparatory School, already a century-old school at the time that was a hundred miles from home. There were just a few hundred students, but they came from across the nation and the world. I studied and played team sports alongside Native Americans, Laotians, African Americans, and memorably, two Bacardi brothers.

Through my time at school I began to understand how my friends saw the world, and I grew in awareness and appreciation of the variety of points of view that my classmates held. Though I didn't know it at the time, my path was set toward becoming a fundraiser.

I went on to the Franciscan University of Steubenville in Ohio, a relatively new institution formed in 1946 that its founders envisioned as a place for vigorous Catholicism and academic excellence. I found it just so. I majored in theology and stayed on to earn an MBA by attending night and weekend classes. The university also provided me with an extraordinary professional opportunity as director of Christian outreach and as a senior administrator with faculty status. Part of my job, though not all of it, was raising the university's profile, which also meant raising money on occasion. I am proud to say that two of my accomplishments over those twelve years were leading the Outreach Division to an average of 10 percent net income over goal each year and overseeing a conference operation that grew from 3,500 to 65,000 annual participants.

The past twenty-four years I have been responsible for fundraising for various organizations, ten years for the Roman Catholic Diocese of Belleville in southern Illinois where I worked with Wilton Gregory, who is now the archbishop of Atlanta; several years at Saint Louis University as an associate vice president for university development; and the past decade as vice chancellor for advancement at the University of Missouri–St. Louis.

During these years I have witnessed time and again the transforming power of philanthropy. I've had the privilege to start many programs, activities, and initiatives, with the help of others. They range from comprehensive campaigns to first-time campaigns, to building a foundation, to developing programs that train and empower people in the field of fundraising.

You will learn a little bit more about me as we move along. I will share my experiences as a fundraiser as well as those of some of my distinguished peers. But *Five Minutes for Fundraising* is focused on you and specifically what I can do to help you find a purpose in fundraising, be of service to others, and help transform our world for the better.

The book is divided into three parts. Part I offers a simple fundraising story that gives you some insight into how I work. Part II contains lessons and advice that I have gleaned on the topic of engaging with donors—building relationships and improving ourselves so that we can be the best at our job. It answers questions about developing and managing the donor cycle, learning to really listen when others talk, and understanding the reciprocity that is inherent in the fundraising realm. You will find guidance on executing donor calls in Part III. These ideas are based on my many years in the field, specifically what I have learned from my successes and failures. Each chapter also includes a contribution from another fundraising professional, who shares important insights and real-world experience that illustrates the topic of the chapter. Finally, the afterword, "Why Do People Give?" by Fred Alvis Bleeke, presents a thorough examination of the fundraising field, linking it to three key constitutional rights in the United States that have distinctively shaped philanthropy.

This book is not my first foray into the field of educating fundraisers. For several years, I have posted blogs and videos called "Five Minutes for Fundraising." These bite-size tactics, reflections, and suggestions on fundraising are the basis for this book. You can find them at http://www.martinleifeld.com. The chapters of this book are brief, in effect, requiring five minutes of your time to consume yet quickly help you to improve your skills as a fundraiser.

Consider this a companion to that work. Please visit the website and correspond with me, too, by email at Martin@martinleifeld.com. I find the exchange with fellow fundraisers a most gratifying part of this work.

PART I

A Fundraising Story

CHAPTER 1

Reach for the Stars, Then Go Further

Do you remember August 2008? The sun was shining on our economy. Well, actually, the skies were beginning to cloud a bit. The Dow was in the 11,000 range, a few thousand points below its all-time high the previous year. The unemployment rate was around 6 percent, a percent above what it had been the previous spring, but still not terrible.

Then the bottom fell out. On September 15, Lehman Brothers declared bankruptcy. Two weeks later the Dow lost 778 points in a single day. By the end of the month the index was at 7,552. Investors who stayed in the market suffered paper losses of nearly 50 percent over the previous year. Some who were overleveraged were forced to sell their assets at rock-bottom prices. Over the next eight months, the jobless rate soared to 10 percent.

At the University of Missouri–St. Louis (UMSL) we were in the midst of a historic fundraising campaign: Gateway to Greatness.

Back then, I was new to my job and on my first day during a visit with the university's chancellor, Tom George, he laid down a challenge: to take our fundraising campaign public in the next year. Immediately I set to work with Brenda McPhail, the fundraiser with the longest tenure in university development, to accomplish this task. Over the previous three years, Brenda and my predecessor, Tom Eschen, had raised some $48 million against a goal of $100 million.

A month later, the Great Recession struck. Many nonprofits were canceling their campaigns, because who had any money to give? Common sense suggested that we should tell Chancellor George it was foolish to go forward with the campaign. Or that if we did continue, maybe we should not go public with an announcement of an audacious goal. It was, after all, the first comprehensive campaign in the history of the young university.

About the same time, I ran across an article in which the consultant Robert Sharpe Jr. of the Sharpe Group was quoted. His comments provided me with important context. Sharpe noted that more money had been raised for some charitable organizations during the Great Depression than before it. Philanthropy bounced back for some organizations much more quickly than the nation's economy, and planned gifts were a key ingredient in building support for these nonprofits.

That was all I needed to read. Sharpe's comments confirmed my desires and instinct. We got busy.

I will ruin the surprise by telling you now that we were successful—wildly successful. But let's first look at the factors that eventually led to our success. One was a relentless pursuit of major gifts. Many of these major gifts came from older alumni who had accrued sizable assets over the years. But UMSL is a young institution, founded in 1963. At that time—2008–2009—only our oldest alumni were reaching the point at which they had acquired the resources needed for a major gift and could begin to think about giving back. Because of the limited number of prospective individual major donors, over its early years the university had relied on corporations and foundations for such assistance.

During the first three years of the campaign, three seven-figure commitments were raised among the $48 million in contributions.

Let me be clear, a six-figure commitment is terrific and every gift, whatever the size, truly matters. But we had only so much time to meet our campaign goal, and it only made sense to spend the bulk of our time with the donors who could commit the highest number of dollars.

So, we raised the bar, asking donors to reach it or exceed it. At the time, the university had what was called the Auguste Chouteau Society. It recognized individuals whose cumulative giving amounted to $100,000. If they gave, for example, $5,000 in cash, pledged another $10,000, and made a bequest for $85,000, they would reach $100,000 cumulatively and we would recognize them at that level. But we had no giving level above that, so we created "Partners for Greatness," which recognized giving at a $1 million minimum, not just for individuals but for organizations as well.

We had another key ingredient for success: donors who led. Among the greatest was George Paz, then chairman, president, and chief executive officer of Express Scripts, the largest company in the state of Missouri and a Fortune 50 company. George, a graduate of UMSL, was the chair of our campaign, and he made eight to ten visits with our team that were catalytic in helping us to reach our goal.

We followed this strategizing with a lot of meetings and solicitations. We will talk more about our team's fundraising approach, as well as how others do it, in later chapters. But I want to mention here the power of gift announcements. Obviously, a major gift is a wonderful benefit to the university in and of itself. But an announcement has the potential to leverage even more gifts if handled in an appropriate way. We wanted alumni and those who had taken a strong interest in the university to know that UMSL was raising money and that people were making serious investments in the university.

One very serious investment came from Anheuser-Busch (A-B). But it had to be handled very delicately. At the time, A-B was in talks with InBev, the company with which it would later merge. Just before that deal was consummated, A-B's gift committee met and made some key allocations. One was $2.5 million to UMSL, but because of the merger, the gift announcement was strictly embargoed. During the embargo period, we worked closely with A-B's executives to manage communications about the gift, and they agreed to announce it publicly on our campus when it became appropriate for them to do so.

When we finally held that press conference in February 2009, we drew massive coverage from the media, not just in St. Louis, but worldwide. Everywhere, people were curious about the new AB InBev and its approach to philanthropy. Nowhere was that curiosity more intense than in St. Louis, where A-B was founded and had grown to become the largest beer producer in the world. And, in a few words, here was the essence of the message that drew so much attention: "UMSL . . . $2.5 million . . . Anheuser-Busch." Could you have it any sweeter than that? The news said to everyone: "Hey, something big is happening at UMSL," and we used that buzz to generate even more donations.

Since then, gift announcements have had a significant role in our fundraising strategy.

So, too, have events. For many years we have held an annual Founder's Dinner, typically in September, when we recognize distinguished alumni as well as faculty and staff who have reached significant service milestones. As the next dinner approached in 2009, we began to rethink the event. We decided to focus on donors in a major way by recognizing those in the Auguste Chouteau Society and, even more significantly, those who had stepped up to be Partners for Greatness. We would invite these donors onto the stage and present them with gifts and recognition. We did so before an enthusiastic crowd of eight hundred people at the Ritz-Carlton Hotel. In a subsequent chapter, I will write more about what recognition means to a donor, but for now, I want to emphasize that this reconceived event went a long way toward sustaining our campaign fundraising at a high level.

What were the early results? In the first few years under Tom and Brenda's leadership, the university raised more than $48 million. By June 30 of 2009—in just twelve months, and deep into the Great Recession—we raised nearly $27 million more, a 50 percent increase over our best previous year. That generated more buzz after we announced our success. Both the chancellor and I were interviewed by national publications. The public couldn't fathom how we were able to raise so much money in an environment when everyone's assets had been decimated and people were afraid to part with what little they had left.

But we weren't done yet. We raised money with great focus and intensity through the following September and announced a $100 million goal at our Founder's Dinner. I watched jaws drop as I uttered those words: *one hundred million dollars*. I followed up by adding that we were already well on the way with $83 million in commitments. The moment was transformational. Our donors, alumni, and faculty began to realize how many believed in the value of our institution.

At the dinner we recognized thirteen Partners for Greatness. Among the greatest was E. Desmond (Des) Lee. As the *St. Louis Post-Dispatch* reported upon his death in 2010, Des may have been St. Louis's most significant individual philanthropist, giving away more than $70 million in his lifetime. Among his biggest beneficiaries was UMSL, where he endowed nineteen professorships.

That night, Des was unable to come on stage to receive his Partners for Greatness gift because of his infirmities. But the impact of his presence and his philanthropy was undiminished. Having Des contribute a part of his hard-earned business fortune to our university meant a lot. Having his name associated with UMSL meant even more.

By the following June we reached our $100 million goal—two years early. Some people said, "Call it quits, man. Celebrate it." But as our team discussed the options, we realized that we were fundraising at a pace of about $25 million a year. If we could raise $25 million for another two years, we could, in effect, create a pace, a pattern, and a rhythm of activity that could sustain $25 million annually. We went to the chancellor and he concurred. We raised the goal to $150 million and made that audacious aspiration public.

So how did we do? Back in 2004 and 2005, the university was raising about $7 million a year. By the end of the campaign, we had raised $154 million. Since 2009, we have sustained our fundraising at $26 million annually. That represents sustained growth of 375 percent. Not bad, wouldn't you say?

Moreover, the campaign concluded with thirty-one Partners for Greatness when we had just three in the initial three years. The campaign totaled 136 Auguste Chouteau Society members and 55,000 donors overall.

If there is a lesson to be learned here, it's that you should never be driven by circumstances. In this case, it was the Great Recession. That event drove many into bankruptcy and despair. But by not allowing ourselves to be driven by that event, and instead thinking of ourselves, our staff, and our organization as drivers of our own events, we were able to create an environment in which everyone was inspired to jump on board and soar to a better, more promising place.

My former colleague, Brenda McPhail, who served as our associate vice chancellor of university development throughout the campaign, has some wisdom of her own to share on this topic. Brenda's efforts were indispensable to UMSL's fundraising success and I relied on her not just for her diligence, but for her wise counsel as well.

• • •

"In large part, I believe our success was due to our focus on donor-centered cultivation and stewardship. During my years as a major gift fundraiser, I have come to realize that everyone who contributes significant resources to an

organization has a desire to leave the world a better place. This is true for individuals, foundations, and corporations. The closer we, as fundraisers, can align our organizations' needs to the dreams and aspirations of our donors, the more significant their gifts will be.

The secret to donor-centered success is listening. One of the joys of being a fundraiser is the opportunity to develop relationships with interesting people who share a commitment to our organization's mission. If we are doing our job, every interaction with a donor teaches us more about that individual and the things that really matter to them. Working for a university with a comprehensive academic curriculum and a vast community outreach program makes it easier to find a match between the donor's dream and our needs. Most dreams are broad enough that good fundraisers can make the connections that promote philanthropy.

I have been privileged to work with numerous donors who have shared what was important in their lives, their successes and their challenges, their passions and their dreams. When I express a genuine interest in what matters to them, they are happy to share it. So, too, are corporate CEOs and foundation trustees.

Consider the philanthropy of a Fortune 500 company. During a series of visits, the woman responsible for corporate giving shared with me the company's concern about recent events in the community caused, in part, by the absence of opportunity for young people who grow up there. She also revealed the company's frustration with its inability to hire qualified workers from that traditionally underserved population. She expressed genuine concern about how endemic poverty and racism in our community make it virtually impossible for many to take advantage of the educational opportunities available in the region. She also told me that the company's CEO and board of directors wanted to help change the trajectory of the lives of these youths.

After several more meetings, the corporation made a multimillion-dollar commitment to our local community, about $2.7 million of which was in the form of a gift to UMSL to provide college preparatory training for underserved high school students and to fund scholarships to assist many of those same students in enrolling and matriculating at UMSL. But the company's dream did not stop there. Their gift included financial support for academic counseling, tutoring, and whatever support services might be required to help these students graduate and pursue and achieve their dreams.

In addition, the company and its employees are committed to providing one-on-one professional mentoring to each student in the program and offering paid internships to students when they complete their freshman year.

We listened to the concerns of these corporate leaders for our community and heard their dreams about what the future might hold for the children growing up here. Together we were able to fashion a partnership that allows them to proactively improve our community through provid-

ing significant resources to UMSL in support of our shared mission.

Another example is the couple who heard about UMSL's endowed professorship program whereby each professor is partnered with one or more community organizations. The resulting collaboration serves the interests of both the university and the community organization. This couple had long supported a small not-for-profit that provided cultural enrichment programs to children in underserved areas. Their dream was to find a way to sustain and grow that organization in terms of its reach and impact.

They called to learn more. We met on several occasions to clarify their goals and align them with those of the university. Their first gift to UMSL was $550,000. For the next few years, we met on a regular basis as they watched their vision come to fruition. We developed a strong relationship and they began to talk about their other passions, particularly those that aligned with the university. Today, they have contributed more than $2.6 million to underwrite study abroad, support the university library, and provide scholarships to language majors.

There are no shortcuts to fundraising success. It is hard work that requires commitment and passion on the part of both fundraisers and donors. If as a fundraiser you are willing to put in the time and effort to get to know donors, you will uncover their dreams for the future. When you can align the donor's dream with the organization's needs, you will produce positive results and succeed."

• • •

The UMSL story that Brenda and I outline and reflect upon is representative of countless stories of organizations that have raised extraordinary funds in support of worthy goals. When conviction and passion about the organization's missions are combined with a fundraising plan and a major gifts strategy that offers meaningful engagement for donors, you can realize great results.

PART II

Engaging with Donors

CHAPTER 2

Facilitators of Philanthropy

Major gift fundraisers are facilitators of philanthropy. The simplest definition of a facilitator is someone who helps others get things done. As fundraisers we connect our donors to the goals of our organizations. We assure that donors' investments in our organization are meaningful and impactful. That, in turn, leads to greater satisfaction for the donors. Often, they will make larger commitments because of that alignment.

Facilitation requires flexibility. We may approach a solicitation with an idea of how best a donor can support the goals of our organization, but our concepts may not align with a donor's interests even if he or she loves our institution.

During the Gateway for Greatness campaign, our team met with David Farr, chairman and CEO of Emerson. Emerson is a multinational corporation headquartered in Ferguson, Missouri, not far from our campus. Leading up to the visit, I connected with Bob Cox, the Emerson executive who coordinated corporate philanthropy at the time. He thought that David would be open to a proposal for one of the capital projects in our campaign—either a new facility in Grand Center, the arts and entertainment district in St. Louis, or a new building and complex for our College of Business Administration.

When the meeting day arrived, I accompanied Chancellor Tom George and George Paz, the Express Scripts CEO who chaired our campaign, on the visit. Paz spoke persuasively about the value of our university and how both he and his company had been financially supportive. Next, Chancellor George talked about the positive momentum that had been building at the university because of its academic achievements, community-focused efforts, and successful alumni.

Finally, David Farr asked, "Well, what can I do for you?" It was my turn. I brought up the building in Grand Center, but he declined because Emerson already had commitments in the district. Then I brought up the business school building. "No, in fact," he said, "I'm really not interested in bricks and mortar. What else do you have?"

It is always good to have several priorities in mind when you visit a donor. So, I brought up a conversation that we had had recently with AT&T Missouri president Dave Nichols about developing a STEM scholarship program for first-generation and/or underrepresented college students. Nichols had grown very interested in the idea and said that if we put together a proposal, he would take it to the AT&T Foundation, which he subsequently did. Ultimately, we received $500,000 from AT&T for the program.

When we shared this idea with David Farr, he became excited as well. He asked us to submit a formal proposal, since the program aligned very well with the company's philanthropic priorities. His board agreed to support UMSL with a lead gift of $1.5 million toward a $10 million endowment goal. Soon after, we began admitting students to the program because of Emerson's gift as well as the other gifts from companies and individuals in the region that Emerson's contribution had stimulated.

Over time and through effective stewardship and ongoing engagement with Emerson, the company's leadership was pleased with the results that were unfolding. Sometime later, when Emerson decided it needed to address a number of issues in Ferguson, where the company's headquarters were located, they collaborated with UMSL to establish another $1.5 million scholarship program. Based on their experiences with the STEM scholarship program, Emerson's leadership trusted that we would deliver life-changing opportunities to the young people in our community. The results were very exciting.

When fundraisers align the priorities of our organizations with the interests of the donors, we play a crucial and privileged role in making transformational gifts happen. We help donors make an impact through their philanthropic commitments, which can make the world better and improve the lives of others. As facilitators, we are in the middle of the conversation, but it's all about the donor and the organization we represent. In playing this critical role in the gift process, we can derive great satisfaction. We are facilitators of philanthropy.

Birgit Smith Burton is one of those people who is helping to make our world a better place. Birgit is executive director of foundation relations at Georgia Institute of Technology in Atlanta, where she has helped raise hundreds of millions of dollars over the past two decades. Here she talks about balancing the heart and the head as a facilitator of philanthropy.

• • •

"The fundraising landscape is rapidly changing, and development professionals are facing many new challenges. With well over a million nonprofit organizations competing for charitable dollars, the task of acquiring new donors and upgrading existing ones is becoming more difficult. These demands necessitate more intentional tactics when fundraising.

The science of fundraising is the ability to gather and analyze data to know whom to engage and how they should be engaged. As I think about my job of being a facilitator of philanthropy, I think about how important it is to be smarter in my approach to major donor fundraising by balancing the art and the science of fundraising: balancing the heart and the head of my work.

The art of fundraising is in knowing how to engage donors through great storytelling and relationships. I love using storytelling to engage donors. Storytelling is built around a compelling vision that inspires and presents a case for support in a way that motivates donors to be willing to support a cause. However, fundraising professionals must have the skills to communicate passionately and authentically, creating an emotional connection between a donor and the cause.

One of my favorite opportunities to tell a story involves the Klemis Kitchen at Georgia Tech and a niece of a Georgia Tech alum—I'll call her Eileen. Eileen was managing the charitable money of her uncle, who was deceased. I had known from previous conversations and doing my homework that she cared passionately about people in need. I also knew that she wanted to give to Georgia Tech in her uncle's name.

Klemis Kitchen is a fund that provides meals to students who face hunger. It was founded upon the legacy of Tommy Klemis, the owner of Junior's Grill, a popular restaurant and gathering place on campus for sixty years. Klemis was known for serving students at Junior's whether they were able to pay for a meal or not, being more concerned with students' well-being than with his own profit. His generosity and commitment to helping students, especially those in need, is the idea and impetus behind Klemis Kitchen.

When I made plans to share the story of Klemis Kitchen with Eileen, I knew that an important skill in storytelling is the ability to put the listener into the story. So, I planned to tell the story around lunch. While completing this delicious meal at a restaurant in an affluent section of town, I started the story.

"Eileen, can you imagine being a student who is thrilled beyond words to be accepted at Georgia Tech and the pride you know your family feels for this accomplishment? Your uncle may have felt this same pride." She smiled, and I continued, "Your family sends you off to school having struggled to pay your tuition and books through scholarships, loans, and savings. But you have very little money left over for your meals. You think that you can be frugal and make it work. But you have no idea what you are about to face."

Eileen's eyes widened, and she leaned in. I shared with her the surprising number of students who don't have the funds they need to eat, and we're not talking about the late-night pizza run when a group of kids put their quarters together to get a large pie to devour while they are studying. There are students whose families can't afford a meal plan and struggle to eat even just one meal every day.

Eileen appreciated the story and wanted more information right away. She felt the urgency of the need. She struggled to imagine trying to complete schoolwork on an empty stomach. This is just the type of program she wanted to support, and I successfully delivered it to her.

This is our job as fundraisers: being the architect who matches interests with opportunities."

• • •

As this story about Eileen illustrates, to facilitate philanthropy successfully, we must utilize both our head and our heart. Careful preparation and thoughtful execution leads to great results for our donors and our organizations.

CHAPTER 3

Fundraising from 30,000 Feet

When my wife, Ellen, and I made a trip to Morelia, Mexico, we flew to get there. I sat in a window seat and looked out over the countryside. It was a sunny day, which allowed me to gaze upon towns and cities, farms, ranches, hills, mountains, lakes, rivers—all of which provided me with a sense of gratitude. It also caused me to reflect on this work that we do. Getting above and looking beyond the daily grind: it's what I call fundraising from 30,000 feet.

As fundraisers, we get to work with some of the most wonderful people on the planet. The donors we are privileged to work with are deeply caring people of great generosity. They have a strong sense of stewardship. They understand that they are on this planet for a given length of time and they have a sense of responsibility about using their resources wisely to produce the greatest impact possible.

We have the opportunity to engage with these people daily, and we are richer for it. For my own part, donors inspire me to do my job better and to be a better human being. How fortunate I am—how fortunate we are—to collaborate with such wonderful people.

Second, I like to think of this as a sacred profession that we share. Yes, we deal in the real world, yet we are working with people, with their deepest motivations, their greatest hopes and desires. We must deal with stocks and bonds and properties, as do our donors, yet all of this is only the transactional part of how we change the world and make it a better place for others.

As I watch donors make these significant contributions, they are seemingly transformed before my eyes. Sometimes it's as if the act of philanthropy ennobles them. Their souls, as it were, expand and grow greater because they are taking their eyes off themselves and putting their focus on others.

Someone suggested to me once that I was involved in a helping profession. When I think of helping professions I think of nurses, physicians, psychiatrists, psychologists, and physical therapists. I once had work done on my shoulders and I know the value of physical therapists, chiropractors, and the like. But as I thought about fundraisers as helpers, it dawned on me: we are. I had to say, this is so true. Because it's our job, our opportunity, our service to think about how to help others to become greater.

We are donor-centric. At our best, we are less about transactions and more about bringing deeper involvement and engagement to donors. Yes, people make gifts. And yes, there are transactional dimensions to this work. But that's not the goal; bringing those resources to have the greatest impact possible is. So, our work is not to focus on ourselves as fundraisers, but to focus on our donors and how they can make a difference. We are present to act as a catalyst, to invite the donor to join our mission so that together we can have a significant impact on this world around us.

Sometimes we have the privilege to awaken philanthropy in people. I work at a university that is relatively young—now just fifty-five years old. Some of our alumni are only beginning to accumulate significant wealth and think about philanthropy. To help facilitate their first meaningful philanthropic experience is simply an extraordinary experience for a fundraiser.

Flying at 30,000 feet allows us to think about what is most important. Most days we are in the trenches trying to raise money, which requires terrific grit. But we must rise above it, look down, and think about the big picture. I invite you to think about fundraising from 30,000 feet. It can inspire you to keep moving forward in the best ways possible.

Dick Jung is a very wise man, a friend, and a contributor as a member of UMSL's Chancellor's Council. He has most recently served as executive director of the Association of Independent Schools of Greater Washington and is a founder and senior partner of Education Access Strategies, which assists independent schools and other nonprofits in executive searches and provides board development, head mentoring, and related consulting services. Dick has found a way to be fully present in his interactions with all the people he serves.

• • •

It is important to think of fundraising as a sacred profession we share. But it can also be stressful. I recall my first major, successful $3.2 million capital campaign on behalf of the Bullis School, a prep academy in Potomac, Maryland. We built the Marriott Family Library for our school. That campaign took a toll on me, and our board members recognized it. They granted me a six-month sabbatical during which I did two things that changed my life personally and professionally.

The first involved taking off the first ten weeks to cycle across the country. That's a story for another time. The second was to take eight weekends over a two-year period to participate in a workshop called "Keeping the Healers Healthy." It was led by a meditation leader, known in the Washington area as "the shrink's shrink." The participants included the area's leading oncologists, psychiatrists, social workers, an Episcopal bishop, families of suicide victims, and me.

The class focused on learning meditation techniques from various, primarily Chinese traditions, taught by a Jungian (makes me smile) psychoanalyst.

Fundamentally, he taught us that "being fully present" is what matters. It is making a connection, whether it's working with the patient and family who are told of a terminal cancer diagnosis, abused children or adults, the mother of a suicide victim, or a person in my field who must run a capital campaign with an uncertain outcome.

In my case, making sure the solicitation is well researched, planned, timed, and placed is, of course, important. The considerations should all focus on being fully present, and they must be focused on the donor: his or her history, story, interests, mood, body language, and other signals.

A solicitation for a milestone gift from Keith Richards (fictitious name) as part of this library campaign can perhaps explain what I mean by, and illustrate the importance of, "being fully present" for fundraisers.

With the "quiet phase" of the campaign behind us, my development staff had set up a first wave of larger potential donors to meet with me and sometimes a board member. The staff had compiled for these solicitations the donors' history, detailed drawings of the library project, available naming opportunities, as well as indications of "philanthropic potential" and possible "ask levels."

Keith Richards, a successful businessman, was among the first to step up for a meeting. He supported a family foundation; his son had graduated from the school; and his grandson, Nelson (again, fictitious name), currently attended the school and he happened to be one of my ten academic advisees.

When Mr. Richards entered my office, I had all the drawings and materials on the table and I had memorized talking points suggested by my development director as well some thoughts of my own.

Mr. Richards struck me as a dignified, experienced, soft-spoken man. However, after cordial exchanges and before I could begin my "ask," he wanted first to talk about the experiences his grandson Nelson had at Bullis that year. As he spoke about two of Nelson's teachers in increasingly unfavorable ways, Mr. Richards became notably more animated. It was time to be fully present with Mr. Richards.

As I discreetly moved the materials about the library and the request under a blotter on the table between us, I leaned forward to lend a sympathetic ear to a grandfather's set of complaints about the school's treatment of a grandson he loved dearly.

After several minutes of ascending volume about the offenses of these teachers and how this school was spending too much on buildings, I could feel the air going out of Mr. Richards's "anger balloon" after my trying for quite a while to be fully present with him. After this harangue, he took a deep breath and then paused for a moment of silence. He looked up. We made eye contact, and then he said to me in a measured tone, "You can go ahead and build your library, but what we need is to keep our best teachers and help them work effectively with today's kids, like my grandson."

I mentioned nothing else about our library campaign in that initial meeting with Mr. Richards, but only listened to his stories about other endowed gifts his family foundation had supported. He then stood up, thanked me for listening and for being Nelson's advisor, and asked if we could speak again at some later date.

After several of those follow-up conversations and exchanges, Mr. Richards created in his name, with an initial five-figure gift, the first endowed fund in the school's history for faculty professional development.

Remember that it's about the donor—his or her story, interest, and intent. And it's about our organization and the outstanding mission we represent.

• • •

Dick and I share a fundamental perspective on the lives that we are so privileged to enjoy. As human beings we have the responsibility to become the best people that we can be to have the greatest positive impact in this world. As we pursue this noble quest, success with our work will follow.

CHAPTER 4

It's Not About Me and It's Not About You

You may be very good at what you do. Perhaps you've even been singled out for praise as a key executive in your organization. But remember, there are no lone rangers in fundraising. You must operate as a member of the organization and not an independent act.

As staff fundraisers, we've been hired by our organization to do the work of major gift engagement—developing donors through the solicitation cycle and bringing them into contact and into an ever-deepening relationship with our organization. We need to see ourselves as servant leaders, facilitators of philanthropy, and stewards of relationships, because it's not about me, and it's not about you. It's about our organizations, the missions that we represent, and the priorities, needs, and aspirations that we can bring into a conversation. Finally, it's about our donors and what they want to accomplish with their resources.

What do I mean by the term *servant leader*? We lead, but we lead our donors with a certain deference. It's their pace, not ours. It's their time, not ours. And it's their development as human beings, their development as philanthropists, which takes shape over the course of time. We meet our donors where they are, and we endeavor to lead them on a journey with our organization, to give them deep satisfaction in their relationship with our organization. So, our focus is to help these donors become more impactful—to become greater through their philanthropy.

As we do this work, we become closer to our donors, but we must remind ourselves that we are not in pursuit of friendship. Sometimes donors seek us out as friends. We enjoy engaging with many of our donors because we find them frequently to be extraordinary and fascinating people. Even so, we need to maintain a professional stance toward our donors. This is important because we must never put ourselves in a position in which we compromise the relationship the donor has with our organization.

For instance, our organizations and our donors won't always see eye to eye. We may have to represent points of view on behalf of our organization that donors won't always appreciate. Something like friendship with a donor can color that relationship and make it more difficult to do our jobs and fulfill the purpose for which we were hired.

In a similar fashion, when we act on behalf of our organization, we sometimes must challenge our donors to step forward in ways that are uncomfortable for them. If we're overly attached to these donors, we may be compromised in our ability to do that.

Though fundraising isn't about us, we do sometimes have to focus on ourselves, building competence, deepening our confidence, and growing in character. We have to consider our vulnerabilities. We don't want to bring our personal needs into our fundraising work; we need to check them at the door. We're not out to get kudos. We're not out to be at the center of things. We want to put our donors at the forefront.

Our goal is to bring these donors ever more deeply into the life of our organization, at least to the extent that they are willing. And we do this by bringing them into association with other folks in our organization, those above us as well as those around us. By bringing our donors into this set of relationships, we enrich their lives and the bonds between our organization and those donors grow stronger and deeper.

These relationships should last well beyond our departure. We are facilitators of these relationships, but we don't own them. These relationships belong to the donor. They belong to our organization. We exist in between, doing our very best as professionals to make great things happen for both.

So, it's not about me.

It's not about you.

It's about the donor, it's about our organization, and it's about the outstanding mission we represent.

Carol Schmidt is a senior financial development resource specialist with the YMCA of the USA. She has more than two decades of experience helping nonprofit organizations design, manage, and implement fundraising strategies and campaigns to achieve organizational goals. She shares her views on fundraisers as facilitators.

• • •

I would like to take this thought process concerning "It's not about me and it's not about you" one step further. Let's think about what conditions are needed in an organization to foster the success of continuously raising significant charitable resources.

As leaders in our organizations, we must constantly remember that a sustainable financial development program requires relationship development, trust, and credibility. This is not just the responsibility of development staff. Sustainable success needs to be fueled by a strong philanthropic culture driven by the staff and volunteer leaders of your organization.

Each organization must determine what conditions are needed to support their own culture of philanthropy. Recently, chief executive officers, chief volunteer officers, and chief development officers from the largest Ys in North America came to agreement on six conditions to continually evaluate and further develop to sustain and strengthen the Y's culture of philanthropy. To see how this might play out for others, I offer to you the six conditions the YMCA is striving for.

First, leadership (staff and volunteers) must be committed, aligned, and personally involved in fundraising strategies. The CEO and chief development officer should make time and be comfortable meeting with major gift donors, prospects, and community leaders on a regular basis to share the impact the Y is making in the community. To ensure excellence in these activities, leadership must be aware of best-practice fundraising ethics and behaviors and develop policies and procedures to support these behaviors.

Second, all levels of the organization are involved and held responsible for relationship building. Plans need to be developed to make sure that the volunteers and staff at all levels engage donors.

Third, everyone, across all positions, promotes philanthropy and can articulate the case for giving. Board and staff leadership must teach philanthropic concepts to those they work with, by providing opportunities to experience through stories or visits how generous donors partner with the Y to help solve community issues. All staff members should feel comfortable articulating a story that shares how someone they know was helped by the Y personally in a time of need.

Fourth, financial development is viewed and valued as a mission-aligned program and adequately resourced for success. The development director is viewed as a key leader and partner in the organization and is integrally involved in organizational planning and strategy. A meaningful annual contribution is personally asked for and received from 100 percent of board members. Staff are personally asked to consider a gift annually, and those who decide to give are not taken for granted. They are stewarded in the same way as any other donor.

Fifth, organizational practices are established to support donors having a positive experience. When someone inquires about donating, front-line staff and reception staff immediately know how to respond and with whom to put him or her in contact. Board-adopted policies are in place for accepting gifts, declining gifts, and recognizing gifts. Donor stewardship plans are intentionally developed.

Finally, philanthropy programs have a strategic long-term focus with measurable goals. A financial development committee or equally effective board mechanism is in place for developing, implementing, and overseeing a formal plan to guide fundraising and philanthropic efforts, including annual, capital projects, and endowment development fundraising strategies, as appropriate.

We should ask as development professionals, what can I personally do from my position in the organization to influence the conversations and behaviors needed to identify, come to consensus, and further develop the conditions that my organization needs to develop and sustain a strong culture of philanthropy? As professionals we must ask ourselves, how during my tenure with this organization will I help develop the conditions that will lead to an even stronger culture that supports increased sustainable giving?

• • •

Carol offers invaluable insights here, presenting the Y's framework to acquire and/or deepen a comprehensive culture of philanthropy across the organization that is donor-centric. These are lessons all fundraisers can use to ensure they remember the crucial role they play.

CHAPTER 5

The Three C's of Successful Fundraisers

I'm a fundraiser, not a wordsmith. However, I do appreciate wordplay, especially alliteration. With alliteration, you can line up important words and keep them in mind. And being mindful is an important part of fundraising.

So, here's an alliteration that will help you think about the fundraising profession in a new way: competence, confidence, and character.

Competence is the ability to do something successfully and efficiently. How do we acquire competence? First, we can obtain it through education, which ranges from undergraduate work to advanced degrees. It also includes certifications that are specific to our field and perhaps a specialty in which we operate as fundraisers, such as planned giving.

Many fundraisers could line the walls of their office or cubicles with framed diplomas and certificates. But a good fundraiser's knowledge extends well beyond a formal education. We are insatiable, lifelong learners, keeping up with periodicals, reading books, attending conferences, and picking the brains of the best practitioners in our business.

Yet, experience, it is said, is the best teacher. We need to be willing to learn from failures and successes and to be transparent and honest with ourselves so we can adjust and get better at what we do.

But let's not rely only on our own body of experience. We can learn from our peers as well. It's important to seek out mentors as a way of developing our competence. This could be an official within our organization or a fellow member in a professional association. We can also benefit significantly from experts we have never met.

For instance, I appreciate Robin Sharma, who is a leadership expert from Canada. I've never met the man, but I feel like I know him through his books and YouTube videos. I'm inspired and challenged by what he has to say, and I benefit from his perspectives on professional and personal development and leadership.

Experience is valuable, and we only acquire experience over time. So, we must approach our work with a certain degree of humility. There's a lot that we don't know, and we can only become more knowledgeable through experience. We'll make some mistakes along the way. This can be humbling. But the trade-off is that we grow our competence. And that brings us to the next C: confidence.

Confidence is the trust in one's abilities, qualities, and judgment. We're not talking here about cockiness or bravado, but rather about something that can only grow over time. Confidence is rooted in tested experiences and know-how. Over the years, we begin to learn through these efforts, and we begin to apply our previous experiences to each new relationship. As we integrate the lessons we have learned in prior experiences from engagement to engagement, donor to donor, and encounter to encounter, our confidence will deepen and grow. And, confidence enables us to overcome fears and anxieties that otherwise could hinder us in our efforts to raise funds.

Now onto the final C: character. Character encompasses the mental and moral qualities distinctive to an individual. Donors are drawn to fundraisers who they believe have outstanding character.

How would you describe your own character? What qualities do you possess and strive to deepen? Some seem obvious: being virtuous, being trustworthy, being respectful. Being diligent and hardworking.

But there are others. When I was young, I was supremely impatient. On many occasions my mother would say to me, "Martin, pray for patience and perseverance." When I reflect on my career in fundraising, patience and perseverance have had much to do with the growth of my competence, my confidence, and most of all, my character. If our character is weak, we will never achieve the great things with donors that they desire to achieve. They need to trust and respect us.

Here's how that comes into play. Not long ago, I approached a donor who over her lifetime had given the university less than $30,000. I asked her to consider a $1 million deferred gift. And, remarkably, she agreed.

Actually, it wasn't so remarkable. It was the product of patience, perseverance, and trust. The donor had been working through the idea with professional advisors, as appropriate, and we had had many conversations. Still, she had some fears.

At one point she said to me, "Well, Martin, I'm trusting you."

And I said in reply, "Mary, this is all about trust." I sincerely meant it; that our work is all about trust. She had come to trust me and the institution that I represented. In this case, it was UMSL.

To use another alliteration, character crowns our competence and our confidence.

So how are you doing? How is your competence? Are your competencies growing? How is your confidence? Is it deepening? Is it rooted in the right things? Are you working on your character to become the very best person that you can be? I encourage you to reflect on these three C's. It will help you become a more successful fundraiser.

Ronald J. Schiller, whose quarter century in fundraising has included work with numerous executive leadership teams and many nonprofit boards, offers further amplification of this topic. Since 2011, he has focused his attention on executive searches in higher education, arts and culture, health care, and social services, bringing to the service of his clients the perspectives of a fundraising leader, an executive team member, a board member, and a search specialist together with a large and trusted network of nonprofit leaders built over more than twenty-five years. Ron shared his thoughts with me, some of which are included in his books, *The Chief Development Officer: Beyond Fundraising* and *Belief and Confidence: Donors Talk About Successful Philanthropic Partnerships.*

• • •

Martin's alliteration works for me. I also like going ABC. Let me start with

Authenticity

Belief

Confidence

In fundraising, it is not enough to represent a worthy organization. Fundraisers must gain and sustain the belief and confidence of colleagues and potential donors. For belief and confidence to be strong, fundraisers must have genuine commitment to the organizations they are serving, an earnest desire to help generous people make successful and satisfying gifts, and authenticity in all interactions.

"The best nonprofit managers and staff members I've known have a deep, personal connection with an organization's mission," says Joan Harris, a generous donor and experienced board leader who supports organizations in

Chicago, Aspen, New York, and elsewhere. "They relate, intimately, to the passion of board members, volunteers, and donors, and this results in much more effective fundraising."

Fundraisers must be knowledgeable about what their organizations want to do and honest about what they can do. A personal commitment to the organization and its mission is a big plus, as Joan notes. At the very least, a professional commitment must be informed through careful study and engagement with organizational leaders. Fundraisers must also know and be transparent about an organization's capability to follow through on all promises made to donors.

Fundraisers must be prepared to represent an organization professionally, knowledgeably, and passionately. They must be equally prepared to listen to the hopes, dreams, and motivations of donors. A good rule of thumb for fundraisers is "two ears, one mouth"—they should listen twice as much as they talk.

Fundraisers should begin with a desire to learn the overall philanthropic objectives of prospective donors. Only by listening to donors can fundraisers tap into the full potential of what each donor and their organization might accomplish together. Starting with organizational needs almost always narrows the scope of the conversation and thus the size of a potential gift.

Several years ago, a colleague at a major university met with a philanthropist who had been a donor to the univer-

sity's medical center, intending to pursue another gift to medicine. After many discussions, he recognized that the donor's principal passion was in the arts, and knowing that the university was hoping to build a new arts center, he informed the donor about those plans. My colleague also knew that the donor wanted to recognize his wife, who had been involved in many arts organizations in the city. It is worth noting that, earlier in their relationship, the donor had expressed great dissatisfaction with the outcome of a prior gift, and my colleague had responded honestly, winning the trust of the donor.

By accounting for the donor's principal passion and personal motivations, and by building on a strong foundation of mutual trust, my colleague was able to secure a much larger gift than would have been the case in medicine. The naming gift for the arts center was the largest gift the donor had ever made, and the university and the donor were able to accomplish something together that neither could have done without the other.

Beyond simply asking how a potential donor is doing, an excellent opening question for fundraisers is, "What are you trying to accomplish with your philanthropy, and how might I help?"

There is a difference between asking about a donor's philanthropic objectives within the constraints of an organization's objectives and asking about those philanthropic objectives even before getting to the specifics of an organization's plans. As I've spoken and worked with hundreds of leading philanthropists over the years, I've come to learn that they are rarely, if ever, asked about their overall philanthropic objectives. Most reported that they've never been asked. Indeed, I've never been asked, even though I've given to many organizations. Even if fundraisers are prepared to listen to donors, they miss out on a great deal of information if they start by talking only about their own organizations and about what donors are thinking only in the context of those organizations.

Fundraisers must also listen to donors' motivations in giving—intellectual as well as psychological. The philanthropic process is often personal and emotional. Decisions about giving affect family wealth and inheritances. Gifts are sometimes in response to joyful experience—for example, a graduation, a wedding, or a successful medical treatment. They are sometimes in response to a painful experience—for example, the death of a loved one or being the victim of discrimination. They are sometimes prompted by religious conviction, and other times by gratitude, and still other times by a deep concern over a societal problem.

In short, fundraisers should begin relationships with generous people by asking them what they are trying to accomplish. Then they need to listen carefully and demonstrate genuine desire and intent to help the donors. In doing so, fundraisers will help donors give in effective as well as satisfying ways, leading to larger gifts for their organizations and for society overall.

Building relationships involves finding points of connection. Some of those will be points of connection between the donor's passions and the organization's strategic plans. But some will be points of connection between the donor and the people leading and doing the work of the organization, possibly including the fundraiser assigned to the donor. Through listening, fundraisers establish and support authentic relationships—relationships built on mutual respect and trust.

Donors want to talk to real people—people who listen, sympathize, empathize, and genuinely want donors to succeed in helping the organizations they are supporting and/or helping society because of their giving. They don't want to hear "institution speak" or sales pitches. They would rather see passion, integrity, experiences, and even flaws, than see only—as many donors have characterized fundraisers to me—a one-dimensional, one-note professional.

Fundraisers must not insult donor intelligence or condescend by avoiding complicated or controversial topics. They don't need to air dirty laundry unnecessarily, but if donors are aware of disagreement among key leaders on how to proceed, glossing over internal challenges will only diminish confidence in fundraisers and their organizations.

Potential donors who have felt ignored or marginalized by an organization will likely be more skeptical that organizational representatives are truly prepared to listen to their concerns and their philanthropic objectives. Those who have experienced inauthenticity in the past will have heightened sensitivity and will pick up on inauthentic remarks or behavior more readily than others. Fundraisers must be prepared for active listening and be ready to invest time and care in establishing a relationship that is authentic and that potential donors experience as genuine, before jumping into gift conversations.

• • •

The question that Ron suggests as foundational to the donor-fundraiser relationship is profound and all too often overlooked. Successful fundraisers build trust with the three C's—competence, confidence, and character—and by showing themselves to be more than a one-dimensional being.

CHAPTER 6

Generous Fundraisers

Before we reflect more about donors, let's consider you.

As a fundraiser, you are a passionate person. You believe wholeheartedly in the purpose of your organization. You are skilled in putting that mission into words that your donors can understand and appreciate. And you ask them to be as generous as they possibly can be.

You must ask this of yourself as well. Fundraisers must set an example. Doing so will strengthen your passion and your attachment to your organization. In turn, it will help you become more persuasive. As a donor yourself, you demonstrate that you are a committed advocate for an organization about which you care deeply. You are far more than a hired hand.

If you have been a fundraiser for many years, as I have, you have witnessed donors who have been transformed through their philanthropy. They will tell you they become better people, more sensitive to the world around them and happier because of it. This is an opportunity for us as well, one that we shouldn't pass up. By donating, we challenge others to step up and do the same.

At the same time, we will be able to identify more closely with our donors. We will see the world as they do, having gone through the cycle of fundraising just as they have. Like them, we will have to come to terms with a significant gift request. Like them, we will have to consider carefully the financial implications for our families and for our future. And like them, we must concern ourselves with risk, about giving our money away and the consequences that might come as a result. This makes us better able to empathize with what our donors and prospects experience when we make a request of them.

I can think of no better example of this sort of personal philanthropy than UMSL Chancellor Tom George and his wife, Dr. Barbara Harbach. I joined with them in planning to take the university's campaign, Gateway for Greatness, from a silent phase to a public phase in 2009. The campaign called on us to engage many individuals, corporations, and foundations in making commitments of $1 million or more.

During my first year with the university I was tasked with completing the campaign's silent phase. I wanted a substantial group of million-dollar Partners for Greatness on board, so that when we went public, we would generate enough fanfare and drama to encourage the wider community to participate. Those partners would be honored at the 2009 Founder's Dinner that I discussed previously.

Talk about drama. As I detailed earlier in the book, the campaign coincided with the first year of the Great Recession. What on earth could we do to inspire people to give the university a million dollars? I recall having several gift conversations with one couple whom Chancellor George and I had hoped would make a million-dollar commitment. They were reticent because of the economic uncertainty at the time.

To address this type of reticence, and to lead by example, Chancellor George and Dr. Harbach started with themselves. They worked with our development team to fashion a $2 million gift of long-term recurring and deferred gifts. In public university circles, that level of generosity was almost unheard of on the part of a chancellor and spouse.

"I was delighted that we decided to direct our gift to the College of Fine Arts and Communication," Harbach said at the time. "But most important to me was the decision to make this gift to UMSL at this time. Tom is leading the university through its largest fundraising campaign ever. We thought it was essential that he show other potential donors that we are making a significant personal commitment to the community and campus."

This astounded and riveted our community and received quite a bit of attention in the local media. When I returned to the donors we had targeted for Partners for

Greatness, I pointed to what Chancellor George and Dr. Harbach were doing. To these donors I noted, "They're giving twice what we're asking of you. Would you not come up to the million-dollar level, become a Partner for Greatness, and join with them on the stage at the Founder's Dinner this fall?" And those donors responded. They said, well, if Chancellor George and Dr. Harbach can do this, given what we have enjoyed in our lives, we will do this, too.

The power of leadership in philanthropy is ours. It is up to us to be as generous as we ask others to be.

Felicia Pulliam is president and CEO of Create Community. Previously she served on the governor-appointed and critically important Ferguson Commission. A lawyer, fundraiser, and community builder, Felicia offers us her insights.

• • •

When I began thinking about the generosity of fundraisers, a personal perspective just wouldn't allow me to approach the topic any differently than how it's presented here.

I originally wanted to celebrate the philanthropists among us who advocate in their circles of influence to increase support for their favorite charities. I thought about how artfully they chair galas, how carefully they plan legacy gifts that transform institutions and lives, and how their status subjects them to time-consuming, unsolicited requests.

But, I thought about my colleagues. I thought about the way they work. Hard. How each time we gather together it is all about work, all the time.

The folks that crossed my mind work at small, independent nonprofits and toil with small teams. Even so, they have the willingness and desire to support almost any seemingly worthwhile effort knowing that people, pets, and, oh my, the entire planet may depend on their gifts.

Fundraisers are on the forefront of mission fulfillment. That's right. Here we are leading the way to getting the thing done. Most people don't think of the fundraiser as the person central to the success of an organization, and certainly not the north star of the work being accomplished. But, the truth is, that's the entire job.

Thinking day in and out and through the night about how to make sure the organization and its staff are fully resourced to do the very best they can each day to meet the mission—it's all fundraisers do, all the time. A fundraiser lives in the mission, turning it over in his or her mind regularly to assure that what's happening is designed to address the challenge, correct the cause, and provide the opportunities needed. It's an all-consuming role.

The job of the fundraiser necessarily includes the roles of each member of the team. You must know what's going on. Who's doing what? How? Why? When? Where? At any encounter, whether a planned meeting with a donor or a chance spotting at the grocery store, you must be willing and prepared to talk about the work. You have to be cheerful, encouraged, and inspiring. It's who you are and of course what everyone expects you to be.

When you agree to raise money for a cause, you are putting your entire reputation and goodwill on display and offering it up as security for the support you seek. Ever heard that "people support people, not programs or projects"? Well, it's true. The legitimacy of the entire portfolio of work hinges on the stories you tell, the statistics you affirm, and the progress you report.

The fundraiser recognizes the consistency of the work and willingly does it.

That's generosity.

One of the primary concerns of fundraisers is the ongoing fatigue associated with constant readiness, hyper enthusiasm, and authentic concern.

The temporary good feeling that a fundraiser has after securing a gift doesn't compare to the great sense of well-being gained by the donors with whom they work. Fundraisers facilitate that exchange sometimes at a cost to their potential individual benefit. Fundraisers want their donors to experience the satisfaction of giving and using their resources to advance the organization's mission. This kind of helping makes that individual donor feel valuable. Not just that their gift has value, but that they are valuable. This is an important part of every fundraiser's job.

So, reflecting on the generosity of fundraisers, I must consider the time spent nurturing the organization in caring for its people and programs. The amount of energy needed to be present and enthusiastic each day as you represent the hope of the organization, its clients, and your donors. The willingness to allow others to benefit from the giving you facilitate. The strength to stay the course, lead by example, and remain loyal to the mission.

Considering these aspects of answering the call to support good work, fundraisers are indeed quite generous.

• • •

CHAPTER 7

Staying Put

Ambition is a fine thing. We change jobs in pursuit of new experiences, a better fit, better leadership, and maybe even higher pay. But I'd like to also speak to the virtues of staying put.

I know that early in your career staying at the same organization can be hard to do. Certainly, there may be opportunities for advancement elsewhere and little opportunity for advancement in the organization for which you work. In St. Louis, where I live and work, I can get in my car at UMSL, go fifteen minutes in any direction, and come across scores of nonprofits. Someone who has some decent fundraising experience can probably get several job offers from these organizations because seasoned fundraisers are in such high demand and so highly valued. But at some point, it is important for us to settle in and find that place where we can develop our craft and become outstanding major gift fundraisers.

Although some organizations expect fundraisers to raise funds almost immediately, studies indicate that it takes three to four years before major gift fundraisers begin to generate a return on their efforts. How can people develop their craft if they leave before they reach the stage where they are experiencing success by closing gifts and leading donors onward to additional opportunities for meaningful engagement and philanthropy?

To remind you of my own path, in 1995, I began to work with Bishop Wilton Gregory, who led the Roman Catholic Diocese of Belleville in southern Illinois. I worked there ten years, most of Bishop Gregory's time before he was named archbishop of the Archdiocese of Atlanta. Over the course of that decade, I had the opportunity to develop a fundraising program soup to nuts, including major gift fundraising. From there, I went on to become an associate vice president at Saint Louis University, where I spent three years recruiting, training, and mentoring major gift fundraisers as well as doing some major gift fundraising myself. And now I am in my tenth year at UMSL, where I have been all-out devoted to major gift fundraising.

Malcolm Gladwell has written a few provocative books, including *Outliers*. In it, he asserts that it takes ten thousand hours to become a master at something. A master athlete ... a master musician ... a master fundraiser. ... If we work two thousand hours a year and we're fully devoted to becoming outstanding major gift fundraisers, we can perhaps achieve some mastery in five years. More years, even better. But we never quite achieve full mastery.

I remember being approached by the head of a local nonprofit who said, "Martin, you are a master fundraiser." I said thank you, but internally I was shaking my head, saying, "What? What do you mean … a master fundraiser? I'm learning every day."

Since then, I have gained more confidence, more competence. But I continue to learn every day because every interaction with a donor is in some way a mystery. Every donor is unique, with a unique background, a unique set of circumstances, a unique story to tell, to reveal to us. All of that has a bearing on how I bring my experience of major gift fundraising to the fore in engagements with these wonderful people.

That's why staying put is important. Think about the fundraising cycle. We begin with identification and qualification, then we move on to cultivation, solicitation, stewardship, and recognition, and we repeat that cycle over and over again. By staying put, we have an opportunity to work with certain donors repeatedly over time. And during this time our relationships with these donors deepen. We become their trusted advisors. When I call and request a meeting, they don't hesitate to take it. They are glad to have the meeting, they look forward to seeing me, and we always have a wonderful time when we come together. By staying put and developing relationships over time, we may have one or more extraordinary opportunities to facilitate for a donor their gift of a lifetime—the gift from which they will derive their most profound satisfaction. This is a gratifying and humbling experience for fundraisers.

So, it takes time for us to approach mastery in our work. And those ten thousand hours to become a master are especially well spent if we can stay in one place.

Staying put, especially if you are young or newer to the profession, is not necessarily something you want to consider, but it is worth thinking about. I encourage you to find that place where you can spend considerable time to become an outstanding major gift fundraiser. It may be the best way to make the greatest impact possible with your talents and skills.

My friend and fellow fundraiser Mark W. Jones has moved around quite a bit over the course of his career. Even so, he recognizes the value of staying put, as he will relate.

Mark is recognized not only as a successful fundraiser but also as a thought leader on matters of professional development, talent management, and leadership. Over the past fifteen years he has also helped more than twenty schools and nonprofit organizations through his consulting, facilitation, and coaching. Mark serves as vice president with Advancement Resources, a leading provider of professional education in the field of philanthropy.

Before you can stay put, Mark says, it's important to find a place worth staying.

• • •

I was fortunate to start my career at Rensselaer Polytechnic Institute in New York State. I stayed just two years, but I received a robust education in institutional advancement that most people in development at that time weren't receiving. I had supportive colleagues, and I had great mentors—people who were leaders in their profession and were often called upon to lead professional conferences and share best practices.

That was so important to my development. I was the first kid in my family to go to college. I didn't really have any concept of wealth. And that's something you don't learn overnight.

So, two years there was just enough, but in general I'd advise you to find a place where you can envision staying at least five years. And you'll see why when I tell you about my next job, at the University of Virginia (UVA). I arrived at this venerable institution, founded by Thomas Jefferson, when I was just twenty-eight years old. And I was supposed to show everyone how they should do corporate fundraising. In two years, I got a good sense of how a large university operates and learned how to coordinate with individual schools that didn't always want to be coordinated. I stayed put long enough to land a job at UVA's engineering school where, at age thirty, I became an assistant dean for a school that didn't have an established development program. I was given the opportunity to build my own program. I stayed there for six years.

I was so happy. I thought maybe I should pick out a burial plot in Charlottesville, because this is where I was going to stay.

It didn't work out that way, but six years was just enough. I say that because I was able to complete a funding cycle, something Martin discusses elsewhere in this book.

It began my first morning on the engineering payroll. I was in Schenectady, where I had the good fortune to meet with an alumnus and former General Electric executive who was interested in contributing to the engineering school's endowment. Six years later, one of the last things I did before leaving the engineering school and pursuing my career elsewhere was to introduce that man's children to the first professor to fill an endowed chair in their father's name. It took that long to complete the funding cycle.

If I had left my position in three years, I never would have been able to complete that gift. Now it's possible someone would have, but we both would have missed out on the advantages that come with getting to know a donor deeply, understanding what makes that person tick, and developing a course of action that is at once gratifying to the donor—at half a million dollars over a period of years, this was his gift of a lifetime—and meaningful to your institution, its faculty, and its students. If you hop around, you simply cannot be part of that arc of achievement.

A variety of circumstances led me to take a job elsewhere. At one point, I hoped to become a college president. That did not prove possible, but now I'm happily ensconced at a job where I can help facilitate philanthropy at campuses nationwide. In almost every case, I was able to stay in positions long enough to learn valuable lessons and add to a list of accomplishments. And these days I find myself talking to universities about what they can do to nurture development officers, so they will decide that it's best for them to stay put.

• • •

Mark's story encapsulates the focus of this chapter so well. Fundraisers who stay put help to strengthen our field and lead to more and larger gifts to the benefit of many and to the personal satisfaction of donors.

CHAPTER 8

Facets of Leadership in Major Gift Fundraising

Fundraisers are often seen as people who play a supporting role.

But we also are leaders.

First, we demonstrate leadership through our competence and our credibility. As fundraisers, we influence the future; we encourage others to be greater. In fact, when we bring our passion and our conviction to others, we inspire them to become better people and join the cause.

As leaders and major gift fundraisers, we are also responsible for preparing other leaders. At UMSL, the fundraisers work with the chancellor and, on occasion, deans. We help them to be successful. We draw upon their greatest strengths when we go out on calls with them and avoid putting them in a position where they might be perceived as weak or vulnerable.

I have worked with Chancellor Tom George for ten years now, and we've developed a kind of one-two punch.

The chancellor will come and represent the university in a donor visit by providing updates and telling stories. He can answer every question a donor might ask, and answer thoughtfully, thoroughly, and often with great illustrations and even humor. He, in turn, looks to me and trusts me to do the actual soliciting, to bring a donation request into the discussion and to reach a satisfactory conclusion.

We exercise leadership in another way too, and that is by recruiting volunteers and maximizing their efforts. If your organization is like ours, you probably rely on volunteers to help make things happen. Volunteers can help you do this by securing visits, making introductions, and helping establish rapport with prospects, especially if we don't already know them. Volunteers can also offer testimonials, demonstrating that our organization is worthy of support.

As I mentioned previously, George Paz is an outstanding volunteer for our university. He is currently chairman of the board of Express Scripts and a graduate of our business college with a degree in accounting. He can secure visits with executives who are very busy and manage huge companies when they might not otherwise take time to meet. Then he offers his testimony: that our university had everything to do with setting a trajectory for the great success he has had in his professional life.

When I am participating in the visit, I typically avoid having volunteers make the solicitation. Here's the cautionary tale that goes along with that advice. Early on in my job at UMSL, I organized a donor visit with an extraordinary corporate leader and I brought along Chancellor George and members of the Chancellor's Council. One individual's job was to suggest that this company consider an eight-figure gift to the university.

Our group met before the meeting and talked through how we would handle the call. Everyone knew what role they would play. The actual meeting went well except when it came time for this individual to talk about a $10 million commitment. I don't know if he got nervous, but he couldn't do it. I had to step in at the last second to make the solicitation.

Afterward, we were able to console the fellow who failed to step up, noting that he had contributed marvelously in the discussion in other ways. But my takeaway was that on similar calls, it is best if I, the professional fundraiser, make the solicitation and handle those negotiations.

Another leadership role we play is in preparing others to make these calls. We provide talking points. We sit down with others going on the call and we tell them how we would like them to interact during the meeting. We let them know what each person's role is if there are more than the two of us so that they have a thorough understanding as to what they're going to do and are comfortable with it.

We call forth our leadership skills when we ask volunteers to help us by performing special tasks. Sometimes this is a delicate proposition. We don't want to waste our volunteers' time by asking them to do things that might not be of significance or that they don't perceive as being important. If we give them something meaningful to do, it can increase their attachment to our organization.

I'm thinking of one individual we asked to go before the Missouri Senate Appropriations Committee to testify on behalf of a university project. He was very busy, and the task required him to drive two hours to the state capital, wait his turn to testify for about ten minutes, then make the two-hour trip back to St. Louis. He said he would be happy to do it. After his return, he described how gratified he was by his experience. I see this as a wonderful use of a volunteer in which he was able to use his talent, share his conviction and passion, and do something that he perceived as being important to the university.

I have had the great fortune to work with a top-flight fundraiser, Matthew T. White. Matt is vice president for advancement at Utah State University and president of the USU Foundation. His views on leadership in fundraising dovetail with my own, but also provide a unique perspective.

• • •

Trustworthiness. Integrity. Competence. Confidence. These qualities are usually used to define an effective leader. It is true that having those characteristics is an essential part of leadership. But just having these traits does not mean you inspire others to follow you. You have to set the example and not shy away from any task, no matter how small it may seem. When interviewing for my current position, one of the senior directors who would report to me asked, "What is one difference between a leader and a manager?" As I thought about the question, I remembered what Theodore Roosevelt said: "The leader leads, the boss drives."

In my role as a fundraiser in higher education, I have been fortunate to work with many deans who are highly effective leaders. It has been fascinating to watch each advocate for their college to the president and rally their faculty around institutional changes. I see our role as fundraisers in higher education very similarly. We work for either a foundation or an advancement department but are assigned to colleges and work directly with a dean. A fundraising leader understands this role and can represent both effectively.

It is important for fundraising leaders to know how to use their time, their team's time, and their academic leader's time. They need to know what it takes to hit their goal and lay out and deliver a clear strategy for success. I have seen many deans and department chairs want the team assigned to them to invest time and energy into events and projects that have little or no return on investment. Having the courage to address these situations, and knowing how to do it gracefully, is an essential part of leading a successful unit. Leaders know what will derail them from their goal and how to address the situation in a positive manner.

Working with philanthropists is probably the most rewarding part of a fundraiser's job. Both philanthropists and advancement professionals have goals. Many philanthropists want to see certain outcomes from their gifts. Advancement professionals have certain metrics they need to meet to achieve success for their college or institution. This is where leadership comes into play.

Negotiation is a very difficult part of philanthropy. A donor wants to give money to an area of passion, and advancement professionals want to achieve their goal. However, advancement professionals must always make sure that the gift is advancing the vision of the college, program, or institution. They have to be representatives of the donor and make sure the institution can utilize the gift as the donor intends.

Exceptional development leaders are able to work with both the donor and the institution. They understand the priorities of the institution, compliance and best-practice standards, and awarding criteria. They also know how to communicate about advancement fees, distribution schedules, and investment policies. They can seamlessly negotiate with the donor and the institution to make sure that both the donor's intent and the priorities of the area they are representing are achieved. They have the courage to ask, and answer, hard questions. Development leaders can negotiate a gift knowing the values of both parties and achieve their goals and metrics by being true leaders.

Great leaders embrace all tasks and lead by example. They are not too big for any chore and do not need to be asked to help. They are the first ones at the event and do not leave until all tasks are completed. One of the presidents I have been fortunate to work with was often seen after events, cleaning up alongside the cleaning crew and other staff. He set the tone for what was expected and showed that he valued and understood all employees' roles in achieving success. Great leaders know the implications their decisions will have on each individual because they understand each person's value to the mission.

• • •

While Matt's comments flow from his experience and insightful observations in the context of higher education fundraising, they are applicable to every non-profit organization.

Fundraisers demonstrate leadership in a variety of ways. We do this with leaders at our left and at our right. We do this with volunteers at our left and at our right. We want to provide them with good counsel and use them in ways that maximize every visit with a donor. This helps to assure that we can secure gifts that will advance the important objectives and goals of our organizations.

CHAPTER 9

The Donor Development Cycle

In a previous chapter we talked about the three C's of fundraising: competence, confidence, and character. Those characteristics are what you need to pack for this trip. The trip is never the same, but it's one you hope to repeat over and over again. I call it the donor development cycle. It starts first with identifying donors. Then we engage with them, ask their support, and see to their needs, which is stewardship. Then we start the process all over again.

Our goal is to develop donors over time, so we take them through this cycle repeatedly. And the more often you take a donor through the cycle, the more exciting it gets. You get to know these donors in unimaginable ways and you come to appreciate what phenomenal people they are.

Identification

The first step, of course, is to identify a donor. In almost every case, we start with the donors we already have. If we steward them well, they will be good to us and help us identify others who can jump on board. A good place to start is with board members of our organizations, who almost always are donors. They can recommend others for us to approach. Another group to tap into is volunteers. Many of them are not yet donors except with respect to donating their time. We should treat all of them as potential donors as well. By giving the gift of their time and attention, they let us know they are already familiar with the organization and very interested in its mission.

Recently I interacted with Andy Zahn, chief operating officer for the Scouts BSA, Greater St. Louis Council, and many other executives with the council. Early on, they recognized a major strength and a glaring weakness in their organization. The strength in scouting comes from its volunteers. So many adults throughout the region step up to help boys develop into leaders. And yet very few of those volunteers support the scouts financially. Perhaps they have not been asked.

Of course, there's another huge group of people with resources that the scouts can approach: parents. They are entrusting their children to the Boy Scouts to help them thrive. As we already noted, trust is a great foundation upon which to build a discussion for financial support.

Finally, look at major gift donors who are supporting other organizations that may be at least a little bit like your own.

My wife, Ellen, and I visited a local museum recently and in two prominent places we found two large walls with the names of donors who had given extraordinary sums of money. I couldn't help myself. I took out my phone and went *click, click, click,* capturing pictures of all those names. We have activities at our university that involve the arts. We should consider approaching some of those philanthropists, too.

Annual reports of other nonprofits are also a good place to go mining for potential donors. While searching, take note of how much each donor gave. Are they a $10 million donor? Are they a $10,000 donor? Are they a $1,000 donor? That is a factor to consider as you determine how much time to spend in pursuit of a prospect.

Qualification

The next turn in the solicitation cycle is qualification. Why would this prospect be interested in our organization? We are excited about our organization, but what would excite this prospect that they would want to give to us? Then we ask ourselves, how often does this donor give? Is it one major gift? Five years later does their name appear somewhere else, or do we see a stream of major gifts? Maybe the donor makes major gifts to a variety of organizations, which indicates they are open to supporting more organizations, including ours.

Understanding a person's qualification requires getting to know the potential donor and asking questions.

What is it that we would approach them about? For how much? What would the terms be like? Do we need their support immediately? Could it be paid over time? Could it be completely deferred? We must be thinking about all of this.

We should think about their financial capacity and consider their affinity for our organization.

Finally, we have to consider our own time. There is only so much time we can allocate to donors. We must be disciplined about using that time where and when it will do the most good. If we have precious little time, we want to focus on those with higher capacity who are closer to our organization or whom we can access through the support of a volunteer.

Cultivation

We know now whom we want to focus on and we believe that person has a strong affinity or could develop one for our organization. So how do we cultivate them? Are we already connected with them or do we need to find ways to involve them with our organization? Can we bring them to an event? Can we visit with them in person and tell them our story? Can we leave literature or a sample of our work for them?

I once went to see a contractor who had been very supportive in providing scholarship funding. On this occasion I brought with me a student who was the beneficiary of his largesse, and she and the donor made an immediate connection. This reinforced for the donor the impact his contributions were making.

UMSL hosts an annual scholarship event where we bring our donors and students together over a lunch or a dinner and give them an opportunity to interact with one another. It's very powerful. Look for opportunities to bring your organization to your donors and prospective donors in a personal and compelling way.

We want to engage people by seeking their advice. We also want to ask them to volunteer. Volunteers give more money on average than non-volunteers. The more we engage them, the more they're going to support us with financial contributions.

Solicitation

The next step in the donor cycle is solicitation. The idea here is to be donor-centric. It's the donor's money. It's the donor exercising decisions over their resources. It's all about the donor. So, as we approach a solicitation we want to be thinking about what in our organization most closely aligns with the passions and interests of this donor. The closer the alignment of the donor's passions, the greater satisfaction the donor will have. And when the donor has greater satisfaction, what does that set up for the future? They may want more of it.

If we have done our alignment analysis properly, the donor will more likely agree to contribute. But have you ever had this happen? Someone says, "Well, yes, I'll do

$50,000 over five years for this important cause." But then it never materializes.

When someone says yes to our request, our job isn't finished. It's not finished until it's documented. We must close the gift. And often that is the most difficult part of the solicitation phase. We must follow up persistently.

Now, have you ever had somebody who seems impossible to reach after they made a verbal commitment? You might say, "Gosh, I left three phone messages." You're just getting started. Leave multiple messages. Email, repeatedly. Involve an intermediary if necessary to help you close the gift. We have to close the gift. It's our job. When you finally get that gift commitment, is there anything sweeter?

Stewardship

I used to think that solicitation was the most powerful part of the cycle. There is, after all, the thrill of the chase and the satisfaction of adding a fresh amount to the growing list of gifts for your organization. But I have come to realize that stewardship is the most powerful aspect of the gift cycle.

Fundamentally, stewardship is giving thanks. If we receive one dollar at UMSL, the donor gets an acknowledgment receipt. A gift of $100 or $250 generates a phone call. For $500, a donor will get a phone call and an invitation to lunch. We value every gift that comes through our door and we are thoughtful about the appropriate response.

Sometimes, this can get complicated. We need to understand from the donor what he or she expects. After the unrest in Ferguson, David Farr and Pat Sly, top executives at Emerson, which as you learned earlier has its headquarters there, wanted to be responsive. Our campus sits just outside of Ferguson. The company's interests and ours were very much aligned and it led to a commitment of $1.5 million over five years to create new scholarships for students from Ferguson and nearby communities.

But Emerson's leadership wanted even more bang for their buck. They wanted to present their donation in a way that would command attention in the community. Accordingly, we worked with their public relations representatives to choreograph the donation announcement. Still, there was even more stewardship to be done. Pat Sly called me and said, "Martin, the annual charitable giving guide is coming out. We want to work with you to design an ad that shows the partnership we share and reinforces this announcement."

Was there anything wrong with Emerson wanting to amplify its donation? Not at all. In fact, it was very purposeful in this case because the Emerson executives knew that by publicizing their donation, they would set a strong example for other corporations and by extension benefit north St. Louis County overall.

Now let me share with you a counter example. We have near our campus a 120-acre golf course. It was privately owned and put up for sale. The university saw the value in owning the property, at the very least to protect its flank from development that might not be complementary. We also harbored dreams of expanding someday. But we needed a gift, as it would not be an appropriate use of the state support we receive annually to purchase the land ourselves.

Our Chancellor's Council urged us to pursue the acreage, and three members stepped up to buy an option on the property at $25,000 each and gifted the option to the university. Then a donor stepped forward and said, "I'm really excited about this. I understand how strategically important this land acquisition is for the long-term growth of the university." He and his wife made a commitment of $1.5 million. I don't think this couple had ever given $1.5 million to anybody, let alone in cash. It was a very big deal and we wanted to celebrate it in the most public way possible to demonstrate again that our organization was worthy of such a generous gift.

But Mr. and Mrs. Donor demurred. They had been public with other gifts, but for this one they wanted anonymity. And of course, we absolutely respected this request. Their names will never be publicly associated with the purchase. Privately, we did celebrate their generosity with a small, intimate dinner.

Stewardship is powerful because it is a catalyst for starting the solicitation cycle yet again.

When someone gives a gift, it makes them feel good.

And what creates that good feeling is a biochemical reaction. It is primal. It's all about family bonding. When they make a significant commitment, donors begin to see us as closely related to them. And suddenly, they become our best representatives.

We've had donors who, when making the first major gift, just about killed us. They demanded many details and asked for exceptions and extraordinary conditions. Then, once we thought it was all done, they wanted to review everything and make further changes. Finally, they came to terms. They signed on the dotted line and, sometimes suddenly and sometimes gradually, their disposition changed. The next time we went through the gift cycle with them, it was less about their individual needs and the protection of their assets and more about how they could be even more helpful. "What's that you need, Martin? Oh, I can understand why the university needs that, why your students need that. Let's see how we can help you."

The more you go through this cycle of developing donors, the more amazing the process becomes. That's because attachment happens and deepens. We are brought into a donor's inner circle, and when that happens they almost always agree to do whatever they can to assist us.

Now I am eager for you to hear from Shaun Keister, vice chancellor of development and alumni relations at the University of California, Davis. Shaun manages a team of more than 220 development and alumni professionals who secure more than $200 million annually for the university. At age forty-five, Shaun is a generation younger than me and has served three state universities over the past twenty years. He also comes from a unique background, which he sometimes uses to his advantage.

• • •

I agree with everything Martin has said in this chapter, but perhaps I can put this solicitation cycle under a slightly different lens. I was the first person in my family to go to college. My mother and father worked in factories in central Pennsylvania. My grandparents were farmers.

As Martin relates, in starting the solicitation cycle, it is especially important to build a connection to donors that goes beyond the superficial, beyond the immediate needs of your organization, and beyond a donor's capacity to write a check.

In getting to know a donor, you ask questions about that person, but they ask questions about you, if only at first to be polite. In responding, I talk about where I came from, my grandparents, my parents, and how my getting a college education was so important to them and ultimately transformational for me.

At UC Davis, some alumni are like me—they, too, were first-generation college students. So, we find a connection, even when those alumni come from a different place—not Pennsylvania but from Central and Southern California, or perhaps even south of the border. Many of our wealthier donors do come from some wealth. Still, they are moved by stories of people who started with little (as so many of their parents and grandparents did) and are working their way into realizing the American dream. After sharing my background, I can speak on behalf of our students in a way that feels authentic to the donor.

My point here is that it's important for donor and fundraiser to "get" each other on a human level. That can accelerate the solicitation process in so many ways.

Martin mentioned stewardship as a key aspect in the cycle, and I heartily endorse that concept. In fact, I have a story about how I benefited in the aftermath of stewardship gone awry.

One day not long after I arrived at UC Davis, I visited a donor who had underwritten two scholarships. She said that with one scholarship, she got thank-you notes and updates on how her funds had benefited the student. But for the other, she heard little and she was more than upset about it. As the new guy, I could promise that I would fix that problem quickly. And I did. We arranged for her scholarship students to write thank-you notes. We got them on a video and showed her the performance on her endowment.

She appreciated that and told us that we went far beyond expectations. About six months later, she asked the chancellor and me to visit her in Southern California, about five hundred miles away. She didn't say why. We flew down and began talking with her. "You have commented that your goal has been to have at least 50 percent of your student body have an international experience," she noted. She then proceeded to tell us that she would make a million-dollar gift so that forty students could have such an experience. And she gave us the money within a year so that our current crop of students could benefit.

When the students returned, we got them quickly on a video to tell the story of how transformational their international experience had been. The donor was deeply moved by these accounts.

Not long after, the donor fell ill and again asked if we would visit with her. But just ahead of our flight, the family called and said she was too weak to see us. A week later, she had rallied a bit and found the strength to call and give us some news. She said: "I'm going to leave my entire estate to the university and I want you to put my name on a new recital hall. I want to be the first alumna to have her name on the building to set an example for others."

Our donor died within forty-eight hours of signing her bequest papers. Now we are opening the recital hall with her name on it.

This was an enormous financial gift. But the gift she also gave us came years ago when she had told us how angry she had been with us. It gave us an opportunity to fix the problem and demonstrate that we could be trusted.

Trust is an essential part of the solicitation cycle. When you have it—when you've earned it—the cycle can move very quickly and to the benefit of all.

• • •

In Shaun's story I am especially struck by his insight about the importance of fundraisers spending time to engage with the prospective donor so that they "get" each other. I was inspired by how his stewardship response to a complaint led to a life-giving experience for a donor as her final days and hours approached.

CHAPTER 10

Listening to Donors

Fundraisers are known for asking. But successful fundraisers must listen first.

Listening is the lubrication for establishing strong relationships with donors. What excites them? What causes them concern? What are they passionate about during a visit? What do they care about today so much that they're telling us about it? We want to learn as much as possible from and about our donors because we respect them so much. They are extraordinary people.

It is natural to think of listening as a bit of a chore, as preliminary conversation to get through before we conduct the business at hand. But these conversations exist for us to absorb and then record. After a visit with a donor, I get in the car, call my assistant, and dictate what I heard from the donor. That dictation might include what a donor disclosed about children or grandchildren, about business, about a spouse, or about parents.

I record the visits so that I can be a good steward. But I also record them because I have an unreliable memory.

The next time I prepare to see a donor, I review my notes. I can then follow up on or inquire about one or more of the items we last discussed.

For instance, with a gentleman I visited not long ago, I said, "Tell me, are you going to be able to come into town for your fiftieth high school reunion? I know you said there were potential timing conflicts around a particular business project, as well as a new grandchild on the way."

In bringing all of this up—information entirely unrelated to a donation—I am telling the donor that the last time he spoke to me, I listened. I took what he said seriously, and I asked for an update. If the tables were turned, I would want to be treated the same way. I would feel respected and appreciated by such treatment. And that's how we want our donors to experience us as representatives of our organizations.

Donors understand that transactions are a part of the conversation and that as fundraisers we come with needs, opportunities, and aspirations, and we ask them to join us in partnering and investing. But they don't want to be viewed as checkbooks. They want to be respected as people.

What's wonderful about listening—about respecting, recording, recalling, and continuing the conversations about what donors care about—is that their respect and esteem for us and for our institutions deepens in the process. Put them first and you will enjoy the benefits that come because of such engagement.

My longtime friend Matt Senecal, who serves as a development officer and campaign director at Concordia University in Portland, also believes that listening is a crucial part of fundraising. He shares his insights in the following pages.

• • •

Success in fundraising is directly related to the authentic and lasting relationships we develop with donors and prospective supporters.

What does it mean to really listen? It is about attention, awareness, and our commitment to hear someone else's story; to understand what it's like to walk in their shoes, to get what really matters to them and to know who and what they care about.

The late Stephen Covey, author of The 7 Habits of Highly Effective People, *once wrote, "Most people don't listen with the intent to understand; they listen with the intent to reply." It is easy to get caught in this trap anytime we connect with others, particularly as we meet with donors. While another shares, our mind can be focused on our agenda, our next move, or our reply—in other words, on ourselves. This obviously compromises our ability to listen.*

Self-awareness is foundational to being a good listener. I find it helpful to get in touch, to listen to what is going on for me as I approach visiting with someone.

As a fundraiser, I have goals and objectives. I have to live within a world of expectations related to timelines, budgets, my performance, and raising money. In addi-

tion to these job-related pressures, I acknowledge that I'm fearful of rejection. I try my best to recognize these pressures but not be driven by them—to lay my agenda at the doorstep before I walk in to visit a person on behalf of my organization. Because I know that if I am preoccupied, I won't be able to listen.

Many people believe fundraising is just another form of salesmanship and that what we are doing as fundraisers is focused on persuading, manipulating, and coercing donors to give. If this is the model we operate from, our listening will be focused exclusively on technique, gathering facts, "positioning for the close." My goal and aspiration in connecting with people on behalf of my organization is that this can be an opportunity for a "sacred" encounter that is characterized by compassion, joy, commitment, and partnership. Meaningful partnerships and shared values are what I hope to find through meeting with people. Listening makes this possible.

• • •

Matt's advice to focus on self-awareness is crucial. When we are with prospects and donors, self-awareness allows us to move beyond ourselves, focus on those before us, and be open to the truly "sacred" encounters he describes.

CHAPTER 11

The Power of Reciprocity

Reciprocity is another word to add to our fundraising vocabulary. Reciprocity is about the power of favors, the power of giving gifts.

Dr. Robert Cialdini, a social scientist, wrote a compelling book called *The Psychology of Persuasion*. In it he describes a set of social norms, one of which is reciprocity. Essentially, when we do a favor for another person, a powerful social expectation goes with that gift or favor, and it motivates the other person to give a favor in return. This behavior has a bearing on how we engage donors.

Now, we're not about manipulation. We're not about maneuvering. We're not trying to be clever. We must always maintain an orientation of respect, humility, and deference toward our donors. Our awareness of reciprocity and its influence on interactions with our donors is good for our donors and could be good for us and our organizations as well.

Practically speaking, how does this work? When I meet with a donor, I bring something with me. It could be a gift—a university tie, a couple of wine glasses with the university logo, a publication from our institution or a book authored by a faculty member on a subject that I know will be of interest to the donor. I might also bring an article that I came across, or greetings from the chancellor, or an update about a student who is a beneficiary of the donor's scholarship. Invariably donors are appreciative of such gestures. They are often delighted. They are sometimes surprised.

One donor said to me, "Martin, you are always bringing us gifts." And I thought, I'm glad you noticed. The giving of gifts disposes the donor to be receptive, to take us seriously, and to consider carefully what we might ask of them so they might do what they can to return the favor.

I frequently offer to do favors during a donor visit. Offering to do favors is a way again of knitting the relationship. It also creates a reason for you to be welcomed back by the donor.

Sometimes a donor will ask a question and if I don't have the complete answer, I might say, "You know what? I'm not sure about that. I would like to do some research and come back to you with a more thorough answer to your question."

In that kind of exchange, it's hard for a donor to say, "No, please don't do that. I don't really care." Rather, they are more likely to be receptive and say, "Yes, I would appreciate if you would do that." That sets up another meeting. And reciprocity is what facilitates it.

Reciprocity can lead to new donations or increased gifts. But it can lead elsewhere, too. I almost always ask advice of our donors about something that matters, that's current, and that is of concern at our institution. I will take their advice seriously and pass it along as appropriate. This is a donor doing a favor for our organization. I will ask for their assistance in other ways as well. Would they volunteer? Would they come with me on a call to accomplish something with another organization or donor? Would they introduce our chancellor, one of our deans, a faculty member, or myself to someone they know so we can begin a new relationship?

Reciprocity is a powerful concept. We want to go the extra mile for our donors when we can. I have certain donors who will call upon me with some regularity to ask about one matter or another. Some of our donors have children attending our university. If something arises about which they have a question, they might ask me to inquire about a matter for them because they love and are concerned about their child. These are tasks, of course, that we must execute with the utmost appropriateness. But I'm happy to go the extra mile for these donors and my efforts contribute, again, to this dynamic of reciprocity.

Have you conscientiously worked with this notion of reciprocity? What have you learned by doing so? If you haven't, I'd encourage you to think about how to incorporate it into your upcoming calls.

Linda Carter has a different take on reciprocity. Linda is director of leadership giving at her alma mater, Meredith College, in Raleigh, North Carolina. Before that, she was associate vice chancellor of alumni engagement at UMSL. She is one of the wisest people I know when it comes to cultivating productive relationships.

• • •

Little things matter. Martin has conveyed this truth time and again in his perceptive observations about successful fundraising: the foundation of our work is building and maintaining trusted relationships with others. This is not accomplished overnight. It takes a disciplined attention to detail, consistency in behaviors and action, and a genuine reverence for the respect we demonstrate to donors.

When a prospective donor grants us the privilege of spending one-on-one time with them, they have extended the first gift. Think about that: one of the most challenging aspects of our job is getting that first private audience, and that cannot take place until the prospect extends the gift of his or her time.

What are we giving in return? It is my earnest desire to always create an experience that will leave both of us energized about the college, hopeful that something transformational will ultimately emerge, and grateful that we have been given this opportunity to know each other.

As development professionals, we are responsible for maximizing the initial experience and achieving our many objectives. It is imperative that we go through the exercise of focusing on what those objectives are. These will differ with everyone, so when you come down from that elated moment when the visit is scheduled, write down what you hope to achieve with the visit. Taking steps that will help gain the donor's trust and respect should certainly be on your list.

Listen with understanding. But there's listening and then there is listening. You know the difference. It takes practice and skill to listen with all our critical-thinking pistons in action. As we are listening, we are observing: how the office or home is decorated, family photos, taste in art, books on the shelves, name of the beloved pet, how the prospect dresses, how he orders his coffee, or how she treats the waitperson. These are all small clues that tell us something.

When I'm finished with the visit, I really think through what I've heard and observed and layer this intelligence with pre-visit research. I try to loosely define what matters to the prospect. I insert "loosely" because a refined understanding of what motivates a donor comes over time, as the relationship matures. Then, I develop a plan for how I will provide meaningful reciprocal touches that will take place between and during future visits. These touches must be genuine and not manipulative. They must be anticipatory, timely, and serendipitous—from a holiday card to an email with a link to a compelling story about the college that could spark the prospect's interest and imagination. Executing the touches effectively is an art form.

At a previous institution, my first visit with an assigned prospect was facilitated by an advancement colleague who was acquainted with the prospective donor. The three of us met at a local restaurant. The alumna—a highly successful executive who, in the 1970s, ascended the corporate ranks in a male-dominated industry—had done her own homework prior to the visit and had researched the needs of the institution thoroughly. She asked appropriate yet probing questions. She was a seasoned philanthropist who clearly took time to gather information, assess the facts, and make decisions accordingly. My mind was racing with observations and information. Then that awkward moment happened when my well-intentioned colleague reached into her briefcase and presented a beautifully wrapped gift. The prospect's body language immediately changed to a closed position. She said, "Gifts are not necessary."

Be careful. It's perfectly fine to tuck away a gift to present to a prospect during your first visit. Just know when it needs to stay tucked away. There were overt clues in our conversation that should have let that gift stay where it was. (By the way, the optimal reciprocal touch for this prospect was engaging her to serve on a dean's advisory board where she could be an active participant in gathering and analyzing information that facilitated optimal decision making for the dean.)

Martin touches on an important component of reciprocity: "We give because it predisposes the donor to be receptive." The next step in the process is opening the door to opportunities for the donor to reciprocate in ways that provide meaning and purpose for them and, at the same time, truly help advance the college. These giving and receiving nuances are vital steps in building the solid relationship that leads not only to a major gift, but hopefully to the first of many philanthropic investments the donor will make in the institution.

One of the most effective ways to meaningfully engage donors is to ask them to open the door to building a relationship with another prospect and/or to assist with the "ask." We all know how magical this can be when we get the right connections to align.

Just remember, when we request a trusted alumnus to make a phone call to his classmate to facilitate an initial meeting with you, the alumnus is now open to doing a similar favor for the classmate he just engaged. It may be serving on a committee of a board or donating to a social cause important to his classmate. This is reciprocity in motion, as the favor he just did for us increases his reciprocal obligation.

Mapping out individual strategies for each of your prospects is a valuable exercise. Whether it's drawing out a diagram, creating a timeline with scheduled touches that allows for the insertion of opportune actions, or organizing the strategy in your mind, the important thing is to think about and value the reciprocal steps in the journey that lead to a solid and trusted relationship.

• • •

Linda has provided exceptional insights into the powerful social force called reciprocity. To better appreciate the dynamics of reciprocity, as well as the other principles of influence, please review the interviews and publications of Dr. Robert Cialdini.

CHAPTER 12

Time and Fundraising

Time begins and ends with the donor. Donors choose to do what they wish with their resources within the time frame in which they wish to give them. We know this process can be complicated for our donors because many of them are working with a variety of causes, and they have family, professional, business, and other considerations that exist beyond the scope of our interactions with them. As a result, time belongs to them. And they evaluate their giving in the context of their time.

Of course, time is also very important to us. We have very important projects to complete. We have causes that we serve, people we hope to empower, and we need to raise funds to do so. These needs often have a certain urgency. They are paramount, and we are challenged to find resources and partners to join in a timely manner.

While some might consider time an enemy, as in, "time is running out . . . the days are dwindling to a precious few," fundraisers can use time as an ally that we bring to bear on our conversations with donors. We can ask donors to work within a time frame that we propose to reach a goal or bring a project to fruition. Time thus presents a challenge. And frequently we find that successful people enjoy taking on a challenge.

If it's something urgent we are trying to address, we need to talk specifically about when support is needed and why. Those elements are at the heart of the case.

When we have longer-range projects for which we're raising money, we can create time frames. Maybe we find a donor who is willing to match a bundle of contributions within a certain period. This allows us to visit with prospective donors and say, for example, "We need an outright commitment within the next twelve months. Can you help us obtain the match with such a gift?"

As time marches on and we get closer to the end of that twelve months, the campaign takes on a heightened urgency that can create momentum.

We have annual fund drives that correspond to time frames. We have the end of the calendar year, which is when donors with an eye on tax considerations often make their charitable distributions. Frequently they do so with advice from financial advisors and attorneys. And so, we can leverage this time constraint to get in front of donors during the last quarter of the year to ask for their support and remind them why our organization merits their support.

Our fiscal year at UMSL ends on June 30. That provides a reason to approach donors with a fresh sense of urgency in the middle of the calendar year. When we can, we assign recognition opportunities to the gift that they will be making. UMSL's Founder's Dinner in September recognizes the previous year's donors and certain philanthropic milestones that our supporters have achieved. We will remind them that if they are able to reach a certain level of support by June 30, they will receive extraordinary recognition at the Founder's Dinner just a few months ahead.

We need to respect donors and their time. But it is our job as fundraisers to bring our time considerations into play, to see whether we can persuade our donors to work within a specific time frame so that our organization can accomplish its mission.

Sergio Gonzalez, senior vice president for university advancement at Brown University, is responsible for all facets of the university's advancement operations. When he previously led advancement efforts at the University of Miami, he oversaw and played a lead role in two capital campaigns that collectively raised over $3 billion. Sergio shares his thoughts here.

• • •

Martin is correct when he identifies two timelines at work in fundraising: the donor's and the institution's. Of course, we have less control of the donor's timeline than our own. But in setting our own, and in setting an overall development strategy, it's important to know the timelines for our major donors.

Most universities conduct a silent campaign in which they draw contributions from donors who get the ball rolling. In doing so, universities can generate momentum when they go public with their campaigns. These donors are recognized and celebrated for setting an example and for putting the university well on the path to reaching its goal. By the time you have completed the silent campaign, you should be 30 to 50 percent of the way to that goal.

In developing that first silent phase of a campaign, it's important to understand the donors' timelines. If they are unprepared to support the campaign, then some adjustments must be made. The timelines are also important in establishing the fundraising goal. That goal must be both realistic and ambitious. If you know and understand the timelines your donors are keeping, then you can find that sweet spot between realistic and ambitious.

Timelines are important in another respect. You simply must be organized and on time when it comes to reaching benchmarks in your campaign. The first thing you have to do is work with everyone to build a vision for the institution. This takes time, but it's crucial because many people will be involved in soliciting funds and they all must be on the same page.

We also need to expect the unexpected. When I was leading advancement at the University of Miami, the recession that struck in 2007 and 2008 made us stand down with certain activities, as it affected the timelines of many of our donors. Some had to defer payments on the pledges they had made. Your institution may also undergo a change in leadership. This can have a significant impact because many donors may have a personal relationship with your leader that drives their philanthropy. Of course, one advantage in bringing in a new leader is that he or she will bring along friends and colleagues who will take an interest in your institution. And those with ties to previous leaders aren't necessarily going to go away, especially if we have done a good job of stewardship with their donations.

Setting goals and reaching them on time is critical. Understanding your donors' timelines, being flexible, and setting goals that are at once ambitious and realistic will see you through.

• • •

The interplay of the timelines of both donors and our organizations requires ongoing monitoring. We must bring both patience and determination to bear upon each donor solicitation to ultimately enjoy total success.

CHAPTER 13

Establishing Floors in Fundraising

When you think about fundraising, think about a house. You have a basement. You have a first, second, and third floor, perhaps. Put a roof on top of it and you have yourself a home. In fundraising we need to establish floors. We create programs, and often a series of programs, that enable us to establish floors.

Once we have done that, we can invite donors to elevate their giving over time and move from floor to floor. At the same time, we can recognize them for reaching certain levels and for being so generous to our organizations.

As I previously mentioned, when I arrived at UMSL in August of 2008, we had just completed three years of the first comprehensive fundraising campaign in the history of our young university. We had four years to go with the campaign. At that point, we had already established the Pierre Laclede Society to encourage annual giving of

$1,000 or more. By the end of the third year, 425 donors had joined at that level. It was a great start.

In the years since, that group has exceeded 1,880 members. The effort of expanding membership in the program became the leadership component of the annual giving program for the university, and in the context of the campaign it created opportunities for donors and prospective donors to begin giving additional dollars.

UMSL also provides recognition through our Auguste Chouteau Society, a program for individuals who have made commitments of $100,000 or more. For example, let's say that a donor has given $20,000 over his or her lifetime, then established an endowed scholarship for $30,000 to be paid over five years, and then added a bequest of $50,000 for the university. Those contributions add up to $100,000, and they make that donor eligible for membership in our Auguste Chouteau Society.

But when I came to UMSL, $100,000 was the highest threshold for which we offered recognition.

Shortly after my arrival, we created Partners for Greatness, a program recognizing both individuals and organizations that had made gift commitments totaling $1 million or more. In the first three years of the campaign, we had three donors make commitments in the seven figures. In the next four years, we used Partners for Greatness as an opportunity to initiate conversations and to challenge donors to reach the million-dollar level and to join with others in providing significant leadership to the university.

It worked. We added twenty-eight seven-figure donors to the original three who made gift commitments during the first three years of the campaign.

This million-dollar level created momentum and excitement. At our annual Founders Dinner, we celebrated our Partners for Greatness and the members of the Auguste Chouteau Society in front of an audience of eight hundred at the Ritz-Carlton Hotel. These donors inspired others to step forward and invest in the university's future.

The campaign, and with it the Partners for Greatness recognition program, concluded in June 2012. I was perplexed at first and wondered what we could do next to stimulate major giving.

First, we consulted with our Chancellor's Council, the most senior advisory group to the university, and our chancellor. Then we talked with numerous major donors, both individuals and representatives of organizations. In response to their suggestions we continued our Auguste Chouteau Society and expanded it to recognize organizations as well as individuals. Now we present opportunities for significant recognition when a donor reaches one of a series of milestones: $100,000, $250,000, $500,000, $1 million, $2.5 million, $5 million, and $10 million. I hope I'm around to add a $25 million level. Well, while we're at it, add a $100 million level, too!

The point is that this provided for us, as fundraisers and as an institution, an ongoing opportunity to talk with our donors about continuing to elevate their giving. We can suggest to donors that they might stretch to the next milestone to demonstrate leadership and inspire others to follow their example.

This evolution has been surprisingly impactful. I remember one donor saying, "Well, you know so-and-so, they're at $500,000. We can't get there right away, but we're going to go from $100,000 to $250,000 and we want to be on the stage at the Founder's Dinner this fall."

We know that donors, and certainly our donors at UMSL, don't give for the recognition. They're focused on making things happen with their charitable dollars for the good of the world and for the good of others. But, with few exceptions, they appreciate our recognition along the way. We use our Founder's Dinner to recognize them in a public but respectful way. Also, we take steps in our stewardship to recognize these donors when they move from one milestone to another.

By establishing floors, you create a sustainable fundraising program. I imagine we will have the Auguste Chouteau Society at UMSL for many decades to come. And we will continue to find ways to add more levels and inspire people to support the vitally important mission of this great university.

Ilene Novack, an UMSL alumna, as well as a friend, fundraiser, and philanthropist in her own right, has an interesting perspective on establishing floors in fundsraising. After graduating from UMSL, Ilene married her high school sweetheart and fellow UMSL classmate, Stephen. They moved to Chicago, where Ilene started teaching and Steve attended law school, after which he went on to launch a very successful career as an attorney.

As she raised her children, Ilene became active in the Jewish Federation. I'll let her take the story from there.

• • •

I have been active for the past forty years with the Jewish Federation of Chicago, which has long-established entry points for donors. In my work with the Women's Division, I applied that approach to donations of as little as $100.

That $100 really starts a conversation and it comes with an invitation to an event where young women can meet others with the same interests and values. We host a $365 Spring Event, which draws as many as 1,000 women, so it's a great opportunity to meet all kinds of women. We also have a $500 event that draws women who choose to make a larger donation.

The next level is a $1,000 Women's Board Grand Event, and in addition to sending invitations, we follow up with phone calls to let these donors know that they are important to us. We also use the call as an opportunity to talk about their interests and passions and how they might *dovetail with our organization. The participants help us out by getting their friends interested and involved. Hardly anyone comes to these events without bringing along a friend or many friends.*

And we don't stop there. We have a $5,000 event: the Women's Division Lion Luncheon. For that, we bring a marvelous speaker to a terrific venue and we work to make the women feel very special.

Now I've described these events in reverse order from when they actually occur. We kick off our eighteen-month campaign with our biggest event and our most generous contributors to get the ball rolling, to create momentum, and to set a grand example. Then we create floors at the various levels I mentioned to make our campaign accessible to as many people in the Chicago area as possible.

As you might imagine, this structure has helped the Women's Division to raise quite a bit of money—$14 million and climbing.

But it's not entirely about the events. We offer something else that is unique in philanthropy and is especially geared toward Jewish women: when a donor reaches the $5,000 level, she is invited to purchase a Lion of Judah pin. This pin comes with a diamond chip in the lion's eye and additional diamonds can be added with every yearly donation of $5,000 or more. The pin is very attractive, and our donors are proud to wear it. In doing so, she is modeling her philanthropy for others in a quite subtle and attractive way.

I wear my pin often, and not just to charity events. It's a great way to meet people. Each city has its own Lion of Judah pin styled somewhat differently. For example, while traveling you might meet a woman from Philadelphia, Los Angeles or elsewhere in the airport, the pin is an immediate conversation starter.

The Lion of Judah pin is a great way to raise money for a worthy cause, but it also is a way of fostering a lasting and enduring community that speaks to our shared values. We call this Tikun Olam, which in Hebrew means "repair of the world." The concept goes back to medieval times, and over the years it has been interpreted to mean that Jews bear responsibility not just for their own welfare and that of their families, but for the entire world. This is why the Lion of Judah pin and my work in philanthropy are so meaningful to me.

• • •

As Ilene illustrates, organizations of all kinds can encourage and recognize charitable support through giving programs that include a series of giving levels. If your organization lacks such a program, consider creating one for your philanthropic partners.

CHAPTER 14

Feelings and Fundraising

You may remember a song from the 1970s that begins, "Feelings, nothing more than feelings . . ."

Many singers recorded that song, and I imagine none of them thought it had anything to do with fundraising.

But feelings and fundraising go hand in hand. As fundraisers, we carry feelings wherever we go, and our donors bear their own feelings, as well.

Perhaps the most common feeling I've wrestled with over the course of my career in major gift fundraising is good old basic fear. Someone far wiser than I once said fear is useless. What is needed is trust. We must manage our fear so that we can maintain trust in our abilities and our circumstances.

Being prepared, well prepared, in advance of a call is a great way to help manage our fear.

As mentioned before, I rehearse. And I rehearse out loud. It gives me confidence going into the call that I will be able to say what I need to say, ask what I need to ask, and do my part in a conversation with a donor.

Just prior to the visit I take deep breaths. Breathing deeply helps me to relax my body. Often, I will also visualize before I go into the call. I will think grateful thoughts about this donor. I will recall things I know about this donor and what they have meant for our organization.

Now, the other side of this, of course, is that donors bring their own feelings into the call. They are wondering why we're coming. They are wondering what they're going to have to say in response to our request. They have considerations about which to this point we may know very little. All of that creates a certain tension and discomfort in the donor. We need to appreciate that.

But we shouldn't seek to alleviate the tension. All we need to know is that this is how a donor is processing our visit. Sometimes as I prepare my call, I will set up the conversation in such a way as to introduce tension early. It has the virtue of keeping the donor alert. I want them attentive so that when we return to the subject of philanthropy and their philanthropy, they are aware of what I'm asking for and why.

Feelings are always present. And we need to be thinking about that in our preparation, not just to manage our own feelings but to think about the feelings of the donor, and about the nature of the relationship.

Do you have good rapport? Maybe this is someone you have worked with for many years, a donor with whom you already have an established, trusting relationship. That certainly can make the call easier. Sometimes it's a new donor, or someone you have yet to ask for a gift of greater significance, and you're unsure of how they are going to take the conversation. That can be challenging for you and, of course, it may be challenging for them. So, managing your feelings and being aware of how the donor is feeling are among your obligations.

Carolyn Grady has a thoughtful take on feelings and fundraising. Carolyn is chief development officer for the YMCA of Greater Pittsburgh. She is a certified development professional with over fifteen years with Pittsburgh-area nonprofit organizations. She shares a step-by-step approach to managing one's feelings.

• • •

Fear—or as I prefer to call it, anxiety—is very real in fundraising and is frequently experienced by both the prospect and the fundraiser. Good fundraisers will acknowledge the anxiety, prepare for it, and even sometimes use it to their advantage. However, inexperienced fundraisers can become immobilized by their anxiety and will often exhibit behaviors that can result in a less than optimal outcome.

If you put yourself in the latter category, I offer a step-by-step approach to overcoming anxiety and replacing it with confidence.

The first step is simply to do some homework. Few fundraisers will walk into a solicitation cold without knowing something about the donor. But if you are experiencing any anxiety at all, it may be because of the unknowns. So, do a bit of research.

Find out your donor's history with your organization and perhaps other organizations like yours. What amounts has this donor contributed and to what causes? What sort of stewardship has taken place? Perhaps this donor has gotten less attention than others. You may be just the fundraiser this donor has been waiting for to pay closer attention to their needs and passions. At the same time, it's good to remind the donor why they got involved with your organization in the first place and to bring the donor up-to-date on all the great work that has been done in the areas that created that passion to contribute.

Performance anxiety is not uncommon even among experienced fundraisers. Practice your pitch. You can do it alone in front of a mirror, but once you've done that, do it with a candid friend. It should be someone who likes you and wants to see you succeed, but is unafraid to tell you if what you are saying is off point or sounds less than authentic.

As you practice—anticipate interruptions or objections to your line of reasoning. Ask your candid friend to think of some objections, so you can practice. Fashion some answers that will at first show that you appreciate your donor's concerns, but then put the best light possible on what you and your organization are trying to accomplish. Try to align your organization's mission with your donor's aspirations so that in the end, the donor can see that you have taken their concerns into account and have gone some distance in resolving them. At the end, out of respect, but also because you want to make sure that you were understood, ask your donor if they feel as if you have addressed the concern forthrightly.

Likewise, it is important to regularly repeat back what you are hearing from the donor so that they know you have been listening. But add to that a little bit of analysis. Many concerns that donors raise are based on a bit of hearsay, something a friend mentioned, or an item in the media or social media that may not be well sourced. You are an authority in this field and can bring to bear statistics, the views of experts, and, even more important, what's taking place on the ground. You can discuss how those dollars translate into meaningful change in the lives of the people your organization serves and supports.

Recognize that if you aren't a little bit nervous about a solicitation call, well, then you just aren't a human. But sound preparation will increase your confidence. However the call turns out, you will feel as if you gave it your best shot. If you succeed, that's great. But if you fall short, you've learned something. That's crucial information that prepares you for your next call.

• • •

As Carolyn concludes, handling anxiety begins with preparation. The Baseball Hall of Famer Ted Williams had one of the greatest seasons ever in 1941 when he hit .406. That's a hit just over four out of ten times. Yet when Ted strode to the plate, he was confident. You should be, too.

CHAPTER 15

When Donors Say No

Fundraising is challenging work—so challenging that we have a shortage of people staying in the field. A study in 2013 from CompassPoint and the Evelyn and Walter Haas Jr. Fund reported that nonprofits are struggling with "high turnover and long vacancies in the development director position." The study cited many reasons for the shortage, including bosses who make a difficult task even more difficult. But beyond difficult bosses, another reason the position often leads to burnout is that fundraisers, like most people, do not like to hear the word "no."

Oh, if only every request resulted in a "yes." Unfortunately, that's just not the way it is. Donors say no, and the fear of that "no" keeps many people from ever asking them for money. For those doing the asking, a "no" means they have failed, and no one likes to be a failure.

But let's look at "no" in a different way: as part of an ongoing conversation, as a part of building and deepening a relationship. Suddenly it takes on a different light.

When we erase the fear of hearing a no, we can begin to recognize that it can lead to a yes.

Some noes are less emphatic than others. Take the individual who has given in the past. We have a relationship with that person, so maybe that no is just for now. That raises some questions and if we can find the answers, maybe we can bring about a yes. For instance, maybe the donor isn't as familiar with me as other representatives of my organization. Or perhaps the reason has nothing to do with me or my organization. Donors have obligations to their families, to their professions, to their businesses, and to other charities that make it difficult for them to always say yes.

When someone says no, it raises the question of why. We can ask that very question of the prospective donor: "Could you help me understand why? Do you have other obligations? Is there something about our organization that concerns you? Is this project something that doesn't interest you?"

If we ask such questions with respect and listen closely, the donor may disclose important and useful information. They may share insights about their circumstances that we can address. It also puts the donor in the position of having confided in us. If we treat that information appropriately, the disclosure can knit the relationship more closely together. That's how a no can lead to a yes.

Often when a donor says no to you they want to say yes, but perhaps to something else. So, if they say no to your request, maybe you make a smaller request. Or perhaps you make a different request. You can ask for advice or for their assistance in promoting the project. You may also ask if you can come back later and give an update. At that time, you can discuss the possibilities of their supporting the effort, making it timelier for the donor.

Not long ago, we had a lunch meeting with a wealthy donor to our university. We did not know him very well, except that he had been supportive on occasion. We invited him to our chancellor's house for a luncheon. We had the appropriate people present and we discussed a building project. We asked the donor to consider a substantial gift that we could use to leverage more donations. The donor said no, which was not surprising. He explained that his fortune was tied into complex trusts and that he didn't have the ability to meet a request like ours.

In response, we made a related request. We needed to hire a firm to help us design the plan for the building, determine the square footage, and ultimately determine the approximate cost. This study would cost about $250,000. Would he help us with this?

The donor said yes. So, okay, we didn't get the millions we had hoped for from him. Still, we had a $250,000 luncheon and it moved the project and the relationship forward.

Noes are a gateway to yeses. Noes are about building a relationship. Noes are not about failure and noes rarely, if ever, lead to noes forever. As you conduct your business, bear this in mind and let it lighten your heart. Be open to the possibility that when a donor says no to you, it can lead to something more and perhaps something greater, even far greater over time.

Don't forget that a no can be the best learning experience ever. So says my friend Suzy Mink, senior philanthropic advisor for Hollins University in Roanoke, Virginia. Suzy is a master fundraiser, now living in Washington, D.C. She has worked with Hollins for many years, and with organizations ranging from the Elizabeth Glaser Pediatric AIDS Foundation to the World Wildlife Fund to the National Cathedral in Washington.

Here's Suzy's take.

• • •

Failure is the best teacher. At least that's true in my case, and it may be in yours as well. Let me tell a story about a couple that came immediately to mind after learning Martin's thoughts on the subject.

When I was working at the World Wildlife Fund I approached a gentleman of substantial means who cared very deeply about the environment. He lived in Chicago and it was deceptively easy to arrange a visit with him. Sure, come on out and we'll talk, he said. So, I got on a plane from Washington, walked into his office, and made my case for a substantial contribution.

His response: "You must be kidding."

I had completely misread the situation. To be sure, this would-be donor had contributed generously to many environmental causes. But he didn't have much of a history with our organization and I had not prepared him properly to assess our needs and the time frame for a contribution. I had misread him because his philanthropic behavior was with other organizations, not our own.

The lesson learned here is not to be in too much of a hurry. As fundraisers, we can feel pressure—from our bosses, to be sure—but it can also be self-inflicted. We want to show results as fast as we possibly can. But if we don't lay the groundwork properly, it can all come a cropper. When working with donors we need to see the world through their eyes, not so much our own. We must figure out where their passions and interests lie and then tie into the story of our organization.

As Martin pointed out, no doesn't always mean no. When a rocket fails at liftoff, it always crashes to earth, and everything is lost. But not when it comes to fundraising. My rocket failed with an elderly woman when I visited with her on behalf of the Washington National Cathedral, but not all was lost.

You've probably heard of the National Cathedral but do not know all that much about its rich history. Construction started on the cathedral in 1907 with the laying of a cornerstone and an address by President Theodore Roosevelt. Later the US Congress designated it the "National House of Prayer." Though it is an Episcopal church, many events have been held there that have brought together people of all races and religions. It is the site of President Woodrow

Wilson's tomb. The funerals for Dwight D. Eisenhower, Ronald Reagan, and Gerald Ford were held there. And from its pulpit, the Rev. Martin Luther King Jr. delivered the last sermon of his life just days before his assassination.

Many of those who know the National Cathedral and its history and have been there to visit or worship, keep a special place in their hearts for it. And so it was with a woman from New England whom I came to know. By then she was in her nineties and I paid her a call. Though the cathedral was opened long ago, it had not yet been finished. Work on the West Tower remained to be done and we were soliciting donations so that the cathedral could be completed by 1990.

When I arrived, the woman informed me that she had done some estate planning and that her wealth would be distributed after her death.

Well, again I had arrived knowing my priorities and without necessarily considering hers. She was thinking about preserving what she needed for her living expenses. I, on the other hand, was thinking about meeting a deadline.

But after some thought, I came up with another way of thinking about a gift that would tap into her own wishes and desires. The completion of the National Cathedral was monumentally significant. After eighty-three years, it would be the last Gothic-style cathedral in the world to be finished. I spoke of how much it might mean to the woman and her family to see a stone she dedicated during her lifetime. I sent her pictures and it touched her heart. I needed to think about how this would work for her emotionally.

The woman made that donation and was able to attend a ceremony with her family in Washington, where she saw her stone go up. Later, she wrote to me: "That was so much fun. I want to do it again." And she did.

On September 29, 1990, President George H. W. Bush spoke at the dedication marking the completion of the cathedral. And the donor lived to see it.

• • •

Suzy's illustrations eloquently make the point that when we put donors first, working to understand their passions and priorities while educating them about our organization, the likelihood of a gift of greater significance increases substantially. The forthcoming benefits of the gift are enjoyed by the donor and our organization.

CHAPTER 16

Some Gifts Take Time

We need to take a long view when we consider how we relate to our donors and how we can turn noes into yeses, as that work happens over time. One story I like to tell brings these two ideas together. To summarize it, I will describe it as "Five years to get the gift that no one else has gotten."

As I described earlier, when I arrived at UMSL, we were in the middle of the quiet phase of a campaign that we had to take public. Immediately, we focused on donors we could approach, and naturally we looked to the business community. There was one businessman who had come to town not long before, had taken charge of a large company, and was making a lot of progress. He was leading it with terrific charisma and business acumen.

We wanted to get in front of him, but we didn't know anybody who could help us make that connection. So we wrote him a standard pre-approach letter from our chancellor requesting a meeting. We followed up repeatedly by telephone and got nowhere. Finally, I connected with someone who had somewhat of a relationship with this gentleman because they served on a couple of boards together. This fellow wasn't very optimistic. "Martin, he doesn't give any money. He doesn't give any time. He's completely preoccupied with growing his business. Good luck!"

Okay, not too encouraging. But eventually we identified a graduate of our school who was becoming more engaged with our campaign. This alumnus had a relationship with the gentleman we were pursuing. Not only that, he had played a substantial role in the businessman's success. But, as it turned out, our alumnus initially had no luck with him either.

Finally, the two men found themselves sitting next to each other on a plane coming back from New York City to St. Louis. Our alumnus had the businessman's ear, and he chose to tell him about the two degrees he had earned from UMSL and how they played such an important role in his development. Would the businessman please take a meeting with Chancellor George and Martin? He agreed to do so.

Months later, we secured the meeting. We were at that point trying to raise money to construct a building in Grand Center, the arts and entertainment district in St. Louis. We were looking for a company to make a sizable contribution that would enable us to name the facility after the enterprise. People had suggested that this businessman's company would be the perfect fit.

As our conversation progressed and we learned more about each other, the businessman said he was looking for branding opportunities. I responded, "We may have one for you." I pulled out a storyboard showing our proposed building in Grand Center, with his company's name prominently displayed on the exterior.

He broke into laughter. I mean, he just roared. And he said, "I should hire you to work for me." He took the idea to his board. They decided to decline the opportunity. But he took us seriously and you might say the ice was broken.

The businessman came to campus several months later. He spoke to our students. He was so incredibly engaging and afterward we planned to host him for dinner at our chancellor's residence. Great food. Some wine. The right people we wanted in the room to build the relationship. But lo and behold, the Cardinals were in the World Series and they were playing at home that night. He was hosting people in the corporate suite, so he gave his talk and left, and we lost that opportunity to follow up and deepen the relationship.

Many months passed, but finally we captured his attention by introducing him to our new business school dean. The businessman made a comment at that meeting about how he was beginning to think about scholarships and wondered whether we would work with a certain organization in town. We said we would.

We began to do that, but by then another year had passed, and we were not getting any further traction with the businessman. Once again, we reached out to him and asked for a meeting. He immediately accepted, and we were encouraged, believing he must have something to say.

And he did. "We are going in a different direction." It turned out that his company had acquired another firm with its own scholarship program, and they were going to duplicate that program throughout the company. Sorry.

The first thing I said was, "Well, we could be helpful." I explained that UMSL had personnel and resources that could help him design and build and support this program, and do the difficult work of evaluating scholarship applications.

Then I said, "Though I'm thrilled you're going in this direction, I'm somewhat disappointed because I had wanted to share an idea with you that I thought you would really like."

He said, "What is that?" I told him that we had some matching scholarship money but within six weeks, June 30, it would no longer be available. We only had $250,000 still available, but if the right organization would donate up to $250,000, it would be matched, effectively doubling the gift.

That piqued his interest. He inquired about how this match could work with his program. We began brainstorming and he said he was 95 percent sure he wanted to move forward.

My fundraising colleague Brenda McPhail and I went home rejoicing, thinking, oh, this is amazing. But I said,

"Let's be honest. We asked for $250,000, but the company rarely makes any charitable commitments. Let's think about $50,000 to $100,000." And Brenda followed up. Followed up, followed up, and followed up. On June 30, the last day of the fiscal year, the company committed to the full $250,000.

It took five years to get the gift that no one else had gotten. The experience reinforced for me the fundamentals of fundraising success. We need to take a long view. We need to have confidence that we have causes worthy of support and that people can adjust their course because of the importance, the impact, and the persuasiveness of the causes that we bring to them. I was excited about this situation because it enabled our university to have an impact on our students' future in cooperation with a wonderful leader and company. Perhaps it would stimulate future gifts to the university, but even more broadly, it could stimulate additional gifts to other worthy organizations. Perhaps we served as catalysts in helping this gentleman and his company to advance their commitment to philanthropy and their social responsibility to the community.

It sometimes takes five years to get that gift that no one else has gotten. Persistence and belief in your mission are key. Be creative. Stick to the task and good things will come.

My friend and colleague Thomas Hiles has been vice chancellor for advancement at the University of Missouri–Columbia since 2012. Earlier Tom served in development roles at Western Kentucky University and Rice University. Currently he oversees a staff of 165 people and a $14.5 million budget.

As Tom notes, timing is important, but preparation is as well.

• • •

It's true, as Martin says, that some gifts do take time. But some major gifts just fall in your lap and you had better be ready for that, because that gift still requires special handling and stewardship. When I was at Western Kentucky, a donor wanted to put his name on a school by making an eight-figure gift. That was terrific, but as large as his gift was, we were looking for more. Elsewhere around the country, donors were making even more substantial gifts when it came to putting their name on a school. So instead of simply saying "Thank you, we really appreciate it" and putting that money in the bank, we very respectfully followed up by sending him examples of schools that donors had endowed for much larger sums. The donor increased his gift, and all went well.

Sometimes, it can take forever, or seem that way, simply to get in front of a donor. In one case, it took us three years to get a businessman on the phone. But it's a good thing we persevered. After we explained the proposal and how it would unfold, the donor said: "Yeah, put me down for that."

I know that Martin deals in another chapter with the funding cycle, but it is relevant here as well. If we are doing our jobs well, we have established a cycle with our donors that moves them through various stages of development that can take from eighteen months to three years. There will be one group that we are just identifying and making initial contacts with. In the middle, we are identifying ability and building affinity. And then, finally, and hopefully, we are making concrete plans for the gift.

That middle stage is particularly important: identifying ability and building affinity. When it comes to ability, everyone would probably like to have Bill Gates as a donor, because he has tremendous ability to underwrite just about anything. But, of course, we usually work with people of more limited means and it's important to know and understand what donors can do. At the same time, we must build a relationship with a donor that goes beyond a financial transaction. Way beyond.

In our work, we deal with a lot of corporate leaders. Many have a different understanding of the world than we and others do. They are in many ways unique. So, it's important for us to try to see things as they do. Asking people questions about their backgrounds develops that understanding and is the key to building a relationship. As business leaders, these donors are used to seeing impact and a return on their investment. We need to know we can make the case that this will happen with their donations.

But it goes even deeper than that, for many donors may have a particular philosophy about giving. We need to understand their passions and their mindset. I call this "moving up the affinity scale."

Timing is also an important consideration. Some donors aren't ready to make a commitment as soon as we might like.

I think of the great UCLA basketball coach John Wooden, who used to tell his players: "Be quick, but don't hurry." I tell my staff to stay aggressive, but to be thoughtful and respectful. Donors understand that it's our job to close gifts. We shouldn't hide that fact. But it's also important that we say to the donor, "You are in charge and we are on your timeline." That is showing respect while at the same time raising the subject of bringing the donor's passion to fruition.

• • •

Tom's message, "Be quick, but don't hurry," is a great way to close this chapter.

CHAPTER 17

The Long View

Fundraising requires a sense of urgency. We have deadlines to meet and goals to accomplish that require positivity and zeal. We visit with donors and we ask them to help us fulfill these objectives on a timely basis. We sometimes feel stressed out by this work, although the stress abates somewhat with the generosity of donors.

However, it is important we also take the long view. Working at a university as I do perhaps allows me to take the long view more than some other fundraisers. Our graduates will have a relationship with our university from the day they attend their first classes to the day they leave this earth. Friends of our university can also maintain an enduring relationship. The university will always be here.

We can look at these donors a little bit differently than perhaps can a social service agency that is under significant financial challenges to raise money to meet immediate needs. Because we have a lifelong relationship with our donors, they can be generous one year and perhaps less generous the next. Sometimes the relationship of the donor to the university is intense and strong. But sometimes over the course of time it wanes because many of our finest donors support other organizations, too. They also have busy and complex lives, with their interests and priorities changing from season to season.

So, we need to think about our donors with a longer view. And our donors oftentimes think about us with a longer view. For example, I visited with a donor not long ago to discuss a major gift. It seemed like a long shot, but I believed that the concept might appeal to him.

The donor wanted to think about it and to discuss it with his spouse. When I returned, the donor, who is the gentlest, kindest person I know, said, "You know, Martin, this is neither the time nor the proposal that we would want to support at the level that you've requested."

This didn't surprise me. But what was particularly interesting and gratifying was that this donor went on to say, "But, Martin, I hope this wouldn't preclude you in the future from bringing ideas on behalf of the university that you think my wife and I should consider."

So, the donor had the long view, too. He didn't see his declination of our gift proposal as a no forever or a no that would somehow cause the relationship to end. It was a no for now. He wanted to continue the relationship because he has enjoyed it and has benefited from the investments and the partnerships that he has established with our institution.

By taking the long view, I could accept that no. I could relax with it. I could have confidence and trust that I can return to this donor in the future. Or perhaps those who succeed me can return to this donor and be listened to, heard, and responded to favorably.

We are representatives of important institutions. We are ambassadors. We are facilitators of philanthropy. Some of us are with our institutions for decades, some of us for just a few years. There are those who preceded us and worked with these donors, and there will be others to follow us. We have a responsibility to care for and maintain these relationships with the utmost respect. By taking the long view, we can trust that future opportunities will come.

The long view does not mean we have to put aside our enthusiasm and conviction. We can continue to challenge donors. That's our responsibility. But we do this only in the context of maintaining an ongoing, respectful relationship that may bear fruit—if not at this time, then many more times in the future.

For another take on this concept, outside of a university setting, I turn to Mark Conzemius, president of the Catholic Community Foundation for Eastern South Dakota. Speaking of the long view, Mark has been with the foundation a long time—since 1994—and has directed fundraising that supports many agencies focused on educational, community outreach, and other activities aligned with their Christian values.

• • •

Taking the long view with our donors reminds me of the axiom, "It's all about relationships." Developing relationships with donors shouldn't simply be a way for fundraisers to get in front of them. It means personally investing in donors—getting to know your donors, journeying through life with them, taking a genuine interest in them. Listening to what your donors care about and connecting them in a meaningful way with your charity. It takes time, patience, and a genuine care for each donor. It requires taking the long view.

The other axiom this suggests is, "The more you give, the more you receive." It has been my experience that when investing in developing relationships with donors, one receives a great deal in return—most significantly, wonderful friendships.

We hope that our donors will trust us with the single largest gift they will ever give—an estate gift. In many cases this has taken years before it has happened.

Twenty-one years ago, during my first six months on the job, two board members introduced me to individuals who they thought would be interested in our ministry. In one case, it took over fifteen years before the individual signed the appropriate papers gifting their estate to us. In the other case, it took twenty years.

Was it worth it? Absolutely! Worth it because of the joy these donors expressed in knowing their estate would be stewarded as they directed and would make the meaning-

ful impact they desired. Worth it because of the good that is being done in perpetuity. These multimillion-dollar gifts didn't just happen. They required personal investment of ourselves and our time, and required us to take the long view.

My colleague, Bette Theobald, is an inspiration. She sees her work in development as ministry, providing a much-needed service to donors. Perhaps the most poignant moment came when one of the donors she developed a relationship with was involved in a tragic accident with her husband. One of the first people she called from the hospital was Bette. When it came time for her husband to be taken off life support equipment, the one person she asked to be with her was Bette. And when she passed away, she left a multimillion-dollar legacy gift that is benefiting several ministries that she cared about deeply.

None of this happened by chance. It was Bette investing in the relationship. She purposefully cultivated the relationship through personal visits and invitations to events, through cards, letters, and phone calls. It was beautiful to witness the deep friendship the donor developed with Bette, and through Bette to other members of our staff. Bette and the staff were richer for it. The donor was richer for it. And the beneficiaries of the estate are richer for it.

I'm convinced that none of these institution-changing gifts would have happened without taking the long view in developing friendships with our donors.

• • •

Mark's reflections and examples, including that of his fellow fundraiser Bette, are inspirational. They underscore the value and importance of viewing relationships over a long time horizon and the benefits that are enjoyed over the course of time by the donor, our organizations, and ourselves as fundraisers.

CHAPTER 18

Fundraising for Strategic Objectives

Does your organization pursue a defined strategy? Chances are that it does, so I want to share with you some ideas about fundraising for strategic objectives.

Every organization has priorities and objectives. It's at the heart of our mission. As fundraisers, we want our efforts to maintain and extend our organization's important mission.

Some organizations operate out of a very clear strategic management system. The priorities are spelled out and fundraising supports specific objectives. Not every dimension of a strategic plan is something of interest to donors. But much of it is, and we can craft case statements for these priorities and go about the business of raising funds to help our organizations achieve great results.

Some organizations have a tradition of working from agreed-upon objectives. They set out in a very thoughtful and deliberate way to meet those objectives. They are monitored and managed accordingly, and the staff is guided along the way.

Other organizations provide much less direction. How the organization functions, how the head of the organization leads, has a lot to do with how fundraisers can help make such an organization successful.

Here's an example of how we can be creative in fundraising. When Bishop Gregory hired me to develop the fundraising function at the Belleville diocese, one of his priorities was to prepare the diocese's first comprehensive campaign in its then 110-year history.

As the diocese lacked a contemporary strategic plan to draw upon for campaign objectives, I worked closely with the vicar general of the diocese, which is like a chief administrative officer, and other members on our team to formulate a case statement. We developed it through many iterations and projected what we thought we would need to raise to meet those objectives. We hired an outside firm to conduct a feasibility study. And then, with the help of that consulting firm, we conducted a successful campaign.

Meanwhile, we organized a group of monitors from around the diocese. They met annually to review the receipts from the campaign and how the funds were allocated to ensure that the diocese was doing with the funds exactly what it promised to do.

We accomplished many wonderful initiatives and the diocese was strengthened through that campaign. The campaign established a set of contemporary objectives that could be fulfilled with the resources that were raised.

The fundraising function can support the traditional strategic plan, but the fundraising function can also help lead an organization forward when it has less definition in its plan.

A good strategic plan is one that clearly aligns with the mission, vision, and values of the organization and sets the framework for raising funds, which gives it fuel to succeed. The strategic plan itself delineates the goals and objectives that must be met to achieve or make discernable progress toward the fulfillment of the organizational mission.

Mark Berlyn is a former colleague at UMSL, where he served as senior director of development for six years. Since 2015, he has served as a senior director at CCS, a consulting group that partners with nonprofits to help them fulfill their missions. The seventy-year-old organization is headquartered in New York and has twelve offices in the United States and Europe. Mark works out of Nashville.

• • •

There are three aphorisms related to strategic plans that I particularly enjoy:

"Failing to plan is planning to fail." —Benjamin Franklin

"Plans are only good intentions unless they immediately degenerate into hard work." —Peter Drucker

"To err is human, to really foul things up you need a computer (substitute planning!)" —Dr. Paul Ehrlich, Whitney R. Harris Center World Ecology Award recipient, 1993

My career has been dominated by campaign work. Whether capital, comprehensive, debt reduction, annual fund, or endowment, it has been informed by my work within campaign structures and timelines. Whether the project is a feasibility and planning study for a church project or a multimillion-dollar campaign for a large international service organization, I have never gone forward without a formal plan of action in place. And the clear majority of the twenty-four fundraising projects I have had the good fortune to be part of have been successful, thanks be to God!

Strategic plans are vital. The donors and even the beneficiaries of fundraising efforts want to know, rightly so, how the money will be used, how success is defined, and who will be accountable for properly stewarding these funds. I know from experience that a prospective donor who asks these questions had better receive the right answers and assurances or they will invest in another organization that can.

Donors these days are very sophisticated. They often "shop around" for a charity that meets their needs as donors. It does not matter how worthy the cause; if the donor cannot see the impact that their support is having on the mission of the organization, they will go elsewhere with their charitable assets.

Martin stated that fundraising can drive strategy in some instances. I think that can be true within limits. At UMSL, where we worked together for six years, we were donor-centric. We were sensitive to the needs of donors and to working with them within the framework of the university's strategic plan—the case statement for the comprehensive campaign in which we were engaged—to be able to direct their gifts to the areas they were passionate about.

On the other hand, we were open to taking advantage of opportunities that arose for the organization to be the recipient of gifts that may not have been anticipated in the case for support. Still, we were conscious of the need to avoid mission drift. Gifts that come with stipulations that may cause the organization to shift programming resources to meet the requirements of the gifts must be treated with caution.

Sometimes strategy intersects nicely with opportunity. An organization that is flexible can work to advance its mission through unanticipated gifts. However, those gifts must not come with too many strings or pull the organization in a direction it does not need to go.

I found it interesting that Martin reflected on the monitors within the Diocese of Belleville, Illinois. We worked on that project together when I was a consultant with CCS for the diocese many years ago. These monitors were given oversight responsibility to ensure that donated funds were used as intended by the strategic plan. In other Catholic dioceses these monitoring functions have been held by investment committees and finance boards that have been entrusted with fiduciary responsibility. Fundraising accountability to strategic plans is becoming more integral to nonprofit fundraising efforts, even in the church context.

"Trust but verify" is the phrase of the day, and with good reason. Donors want transparency about institutional finances and they want to know the impact of their gifts. This all plays into the strategic plan, which maps out ahead of the fundraising effort how funds will be used.

The strategic plan keeps the development team in a complex organization like UMSL from being pulled in different directions that are in competition with one another. When there are ten colleges and units, each with its own statement of need, a central guiding plan is very helpful to ensure that the overall organizational mission does not become lost. This is as true for fundraising staff as it is for deans and division heads.

Organizational leadership must come from the CEO and it is this leader's responsibility to develop the plan of action to accomplish strategic goals. The leadership style of the CEO will dictate how much input a chief development officer and the development department have in the drafting of organizational goals. An organization that has some flexibility in its strategy can often benefit from being opportunistic, if accepting a transformational gift that brings conditions does not lead to harmful mission drift.

• • •

Campaigns can serve as catalysts for organizational development and growth. In many respects, the extent of the alignment of the campaign with the strategic priorities contemporaneously embraced by the organization will determine its impact.

PART III

Executing Donor Calls

CHAPTER 19

The Solicitation Call

You know by now that making a solicitation call isn't a matter of simply showing up. You must prepare. You want the call to go perfectly, to get a positive response, but also to show respect. Donors give us their time, which is already a gift. You don't ever want to waste it.

Preparation is also necessary because frequently it's not just you and the donor who are involved, but others as well. We may have staff who are participating, or volunteers, or a board member, or even the chief executive of our organization.

Here's what we need to think about: What is the purpose of the visit with a prospective donor? Where are we going to meet with the donor?

The Where

The place can be crucial. I once went with a fundraising colleague on a solicitation call in New York City, where we were to have dinner with a couple at their favorite Italian restaurant. They described it as a small and intimate restaurant. We figured we could work with that . . . until we got there. Next to us sat a group of twenty people who were enjoying a celebration—noisily. We were unable to conduct our solicitation, but, hey, the wine was great and the food was, too. Fortunately, we were able to arrange another meeting a month later when the gentleman came to St. Louis and we requested a new gift commitment. Had we really considered the location carefully, we would have planned the solicitation call differently.

The Who

Now let's consider who is best to go on a call. It might be the volunteer who helped facilitate the meeting. It could be your president, your chancellor, your executive director, a faculty member who's an expert in an area that will benefit from a donation. And then, what will the roles be of the person or people who are on the call? You want to be very clear about who's doing what. Who's going to make the solicitation? Who's going to negotiate what follows thereafter? Are there questions or even objections that you should plan for and discuss with those who are going on the call with you? We need to consider in advance the relationship that our donor has with our institution. Is the donor new to the organization or someone we've known for years? What do we know about them? What's happened most recently with them? I always review that information before I go on a call.

A couple might have said to me on the last call, "You know, our daughter, Mary Ann, is getting married in six weeks. Martin, we can't help you right now. That wedding is going to cost us."

As I described in a previous chapter, I record this information when I get back to my office, or I call my assistant from the car to transcribe my meeting summation. Then I review and refer to those notes as I'm preparing for the next call so that I remember to ask about that wedding.

I plan to see that couple two weeks after the wedding. And of course, I will ask, "How did Mary Ann's wedding turn out? Was it exciting? Did it go perfectly?" And they will have big smiles on their faces. For them, the marriage of their daughter was a magical moment in their lives.

Donors understand that during the relationship there will be transactions, but they don't want to be treated like a checkbook. They want to be seen as people who matter. And what matters isn't the transaction but the daughter that's about to be married. It's the relationship that we steward. Focus on the relationship. Record those nuggets that are personal. Bring them back up during the next call.

The How

Now let's consider the materials to bring to the call. Are you bringing a case statement? Are you bringing a letter from your senior executive or from the board chair? Are you bringing a gift? Are there additional materials that you can put in a pocket folder? Maybe it's a newsletter or a brochure or an article about your organization that appeared in the local newspaper.

Conduct a pre-meeting with anyone joining you on the call. Review the call, assign roles, and discuss the resources you're bringing to make sure everyone is on the same page. You confirm the details if necessary and you rehearse as necessary.

A rehearsal may sound strange and a bit over the top for a simple call. But don't sell it short. When I came to St. Louis in 1995 to work for the Diocese of Belleville, I remember how nervous I was about making calls and asking for financial support. Not just nervous—scared.

I would rehearse as I drove through southern Illinois. (The diocese covered twenty-eight counties.) Again and again I would say out loud in the car, "John and Mary, will you consider a gift commitment of $50,000 for religious education? You can pay it over the next five years if you'd like. It will change the lives of children." And when I arrived I wasn't so nervous. John and Mary might look uncomfortable. There might be distractions. But finally, when it was time, I could say "John and Mary" and out would come the rest of the request regardless of how I felt.

I have many more years under my belt, but I still rehearse in the car going to meetings. It works for me.

While you are preparing or rehearsing, don't ever forget to be on time. Never be late. And if you are late, grovel appropriately!

Then implement the call as planned. To establish rapport on a call I like to refer to "the two Gs and a C." I lead with gratitude, gifts, and compliments. People desire and appreciate them, especially when sincerely given and sincerely meant.

"Well, John and Mary, I don't remember that picture being on the wall. Is that the whole family?"

"Oh, Martin, you wouldn't believe it. Last summer we finally had the family reunion."

"That's the most handsome, good-looking family I've ever seen, John and Mary."

Along with the compliments, bring gifts. They don't have to be expensive, but they should be thoughtful. I was visiting donors recently in Chicago and I brought two baseball caps: Cardinals on the front, UMSL on the back. They were delighted and described their longtime loyalty to the Cardinals in a community that has similar loyalty to other major league teams.

Finally, we prepare to conclude the call. Someone on our team is responsible on the call to summarize and make sure the donor knows the next steps we will take to secure the donation.

Now, let's say things don't go well. The would-be donor says, in effect, "I don't like you. I don't like your organization, and I don't want to give you money." You have a response for that as well. "I am so grateful for the time you've made for us today, particularly given your inclination toward us." You may not be feeling warmth, but you exude warmth. They are the most important person in the world, even if they say no to you rudely.

The Follow-Up

Every three weeks, our fundraisers get together to discuss their prospects. Recently, during one of those meetings, a staff member brought up a challenging situation. She said a number of alumni from the college that she services complain frequently about their years at UMSL. My response was that complaints are a starting point: "Wouldn't you rather have a complaint than no visit? Wouldn't you rather listen to somebody vent because they were so unhappy with you or your organization than not take the meeting?" It's a starting point. We develop donors; we lead them somewhere. They might start in angry and negative, so meet them where they are and strive to guide them somewhere else.

Do you ever come back from a meeting exhausted? Do you ever come back from a meeting and think, "Thank God that's over"? The work that we do takes its toll on us. Personally, I'm an introvert. I don't know about you, but after three calls in one day, I'm exhausted. I'll go exercise to destress. It's important that we take care of ourselves.

But you aren't done yet. You must follow through. You must go through post-call reflections and considerations. Who does what next, in what order, and in what time? You want to get thank-you notes out in a timely fashion. When I come back from a call, I send a handwritten note to the donor. I help the chancellor prepare a letter if he was in the meeting. There may be another letter from a dean or faculty member. You cannot thank people enough.

Jeffrey Byrne, the founder and CEO of Jeffrey Byrne + Associates, is going to add to my thoughts on this topic. Jeffery's firm has partnered with hundreds of organizations since 2000 to raise more than $1.25 billion. His clients have included scores of YMCAs, numerous chapters of the Nature Conservancy, and the Susan G. Komen Breast Cancer Foundation, among many others. He starts with a story about another worthy organization, the Harry S. Truman Presidential Museum & Library, where he once worked as vice president for advancement.

• • •

During my time with the Truman Presidential Museum & Library, from 1997 to 2000, I worked with donors locally in the Greater Kansas City region and nationally. We created a campaign goal of $22.5 million, setting a thirty-six-month timeline. This was after a failed campaign that did not reach its goal of $10 million three years earlier. The purpose of the campaign was for renovations, an addition to the Presidential Museum, program development, the start of an educational curriculum, and operations for the Truman Institute. After one year of planning (including the fundraising feasibility study), a capital campaign was launched.

About two years earlier, around the holidays, a board member and donor stopped by the library director's office and handed him an unsolicited $100,000 check. "I think you're doing some great things, and I want to show you with my financial support," he explained.

We certainly wanted this board member involved with us in developing our case for support. This individual read and edited the case many times. The edits were helpful, but I cared much more about the board member's passion for the case and continuing commitment to the story line that we were building during this year of planning. The board member also assisted in identifying and appraising other donors. In fact, when we were ready to solicit gifts, this board member wanted to be asked for a gift before anyone else. We were, of course, happy to oblige.

Upon arriving for our solicitation at the board member's home, the board member led the director of the Truman Library and me into a large living room, at least fifteen by twenty feet. The Persian rug on the floor caught my attention first, followed by the view looking out over a pool and beautifully landscaped yard. The director and I sat in one corner of the room on a banquette-style sofa. The donor settled in a chair on the opposite side of the room.

After some brief chitchat, the board member stared hard and said, "You know what? I know why you're here. Why don't you cut to the chase?" The director stuttered a bit. I looked at the board member and said, "We appreciate *your time, and we would like for you to consider pledging a $300,000 gift per year over a five-year period for a total of $1.5 million."*

We then settled into the silence. With arms crossed, the would-be donor leaned toward us from the chair and after an eternity that was probably only ten to fifteen seconds, said, "That makes me feel very *uncomfortable."*

This was not what we wanted to hear. Luckily, neither of us reacted to that comment. In what seemed like another eternity, the board member sat back in the chair, seemed to relax, and said, "But you know what? I appreciate you letting me know what you would like for me to consider, and I will consider that gift."

The board member went on to explain that circumstances had changed a few years earlier. He was still making investments in organizations that stimulated passion and had given $100,000 to numerous organizations—but never more than $100,000 to any single organization. Finally, the he said, "I have to go away for August. When I come back in September, I will make a decision."

Two weeks later, the board member called to say, "I have talked to my financial advisors." Two weeks after that, he said, "I'm going to pledge $1 million."

We had our first big gift! With one provision.

"I will get trampled if people know who I am," said the donor, "so I wish to remain anonymous in all aspects of public recognition. However, those six other prospects that

you want to solicit for $1.5 million—you can tell them what I gave and use my name. And, if you want me to, I will go with you to call on those prospects."

We gratefully accepted the board member's conditions and offer, with confidence in our strategy for obtaining large gifts. Over the next three to four months, with our anonymous donor, we called on the six other donors. Our lead donor then just about every day called to ask the same question: "Why aren't they making their decisions?"

The board member's anxiety was understandable considering how major gifts come about in most campaigns. I like to picture a big dining room table. The first large donor sits there alone feeling vulnerable. My donor wants to fill the seats around the table with other peer donors. In a six-week period that seemed like a year to our anonymous donor, we obtained a $1 million commitment about once a week. It was the most exciting six weeks I have ever had in fundraising.

• • •

Jeffrey's remarkable story perfectly illustrates the process to engage and prepare a donor for a large request and then execute the call and follow through so effectively. And because of the deep investment that the donor gave to the cause with his time, talent, and treasure, Jeffrey was able to leverage his commitment to raise many times more. It's a story well worth pondering.

CHAPTER 20

How Much Should We Ask For?

Every fundraiser grapples with a key question: How much can I ask from a donor? We can't go into a meeting with a prospective donor and ask for nothing. And we don't want to go in and simply say, "Will you please help?" and leave the number up to the donor.

We want to make a predetermined request, so we need to think about the nature of the relationship with the donor. We must consider a raft of questions.

How well do they know our organization? Are they closely associated? Do they have a long history of support? Have they not given before? Do they volunteer with our organization? Do they give annually or sporadically? Have they given major gifts in the past?

And there are other questions to ask as well. How much have they given to our organization? What have we given them in return as recognition and as expressions of gratitude? Is recognition important to them? Or would they prefer anonymity? Are they willing to make a gift at the front end of a campaign so that they can be an example of leadership and help to set the pace for success for our organization? Or are they more reticent and looking to follow what others have done?

These questions help us gauge the size of the gift we should seek. Then we must think about our case for support. What program or project do we want the donor to support? Is it a broad campaign with many opportunities for support? Is it narrow in focus, like a scholarship program, or a building or a renovation? Is it for an urgent or emergent need? The more closely we can align the donor's interests with what we want to ask the donor to support, the better our chances for a positive outcome.

More specific questions will help to guide the discussion. What is the age of the donor? Where are they in their cycle of life? Is this a major gift or are we talking to this donor about a legacy? An ultimate gift? An estate gift? This has terrific bearing.

Next, consider their capacity and their affinity to your organization. If it's high capacity, high affinity, you should have the confidence to ask for a substantial amount. On the other hand, if it's lower capacity or lower affinity, you may need to dial back the request.

When seeking a substantial amount, the encounter should be face-to-face. You have to be in front of them one time, or perhaps many times, to secure a major gift. While email or the telephone can be a part of some negotiations, you don't want to depend on them. A sizable sum from a donor deserves your time and energy, just as you want your donors to contribute their time and energy, their involvement, as they consider your gift request.

Previously, I've written about establishing floors in a fundraising program. I have also mentioned how I use gifts that others have given to motivate donors. This is a time when those factors come into play. You want to talk about leadership with a donor, about how important it is for them to join with their peers in the community and become a champion for the cause.

I remember talking with a veteran fundraiser about how much money to seek from a donor. He said, "I would always ask for twice what I thought they would do because usually people would come in at about half of what I'd ask of them." Perhaps this might be an approach to take in certain circumstances.

I prefer to begin with the relationship, to think about the purpose for which we're approaching this donor. Knowing that they have a high capacity, I would certainly reach to the higher end of the spectrum for my solicitation. But I don't want to ask for something that's beyond the donor's capacity. Nor do I want to ask for such an unrealistic amount that the donor might be dismissive because we don't have the basis of a relationship for such a large number.

Also, we must consider proportion. If it is a million-dollar project and you want to raise money from many donors, asking for a lead gift of a million dollars is disproportionate. Maybe you ask for a 50 or 25 percent lead gift, or perhaps you ask the donor to join a group of donors who are helping you get to the million-dollar goal by each committing 10 or 20 percent.

I do believe that there's power in a number, and a large one at that. So, don't ask for a range. Ask for a specific amount. Then negotiate: the number of years to pay the pledge, the nature of the gift (outright, paid over time, deferred, a combination thereof). A large number raises the sights of donors and challenges them to increase their support to your organization. It may move them to reevaluate their relationship with you and the value they place on your mission. Don't be afraid of large numbers, but make them sensible and realistic in the context of the relationship.

Finally, we should be courageous and persistent. Set the number in front of a donor and then watch the donor respond, react, and wrestle with that request. Only then can we arrive at a positive outcome on behalf of our great organization.

For an additional perspective I turned to Larry C. Johnson, who guides philanthropies and philanthropists nationwide through what he calls the Eight Principles of Sustainable Fundraising, which is also the name of a best-selling book and his popular website. Larry was named Outstanding Development Executive by the Association of Fundraising Professionals in 2010 and was listed as one of the Top 15 Fundraising Consultants in the U.S. by the Wall Street Journal Business Network.

• • •

Outside of "whom do I ask?," "how much?" is the perennial question in the mind of just about every fundraiser. And why not? Fundraising is about money, isn't it?

Well, yes and no.

The good news is this: the size of the gift you're requesting is of far less importance to the potential investor than to you.

The bad news is that successfully engaging your investor will likely require a significant mental paradigm shift for you with several more steps to achieve success than you've probably anticipated.

How's this?

To begin with, the amount you've decided to seek is almost always partially or wholly driven by what you need. It's internal to your organization and what you want to accomplish. "Well, of course," you say, "these funds are sorely needed to the critical work we do in the community."

I'm sorry to disappoint you, but most donors really aren't that interested in what your goals are—programmatic or financial.

Second, donors are definitely in control. Principle 1 of The Eight Principles is Donors are the Drivers. Philanthropic investors drive philanthropy and, by extension, fundraising.

But they don't drive it with their money. Donors' personal values, personal visions, and quest for personal realization are the drivers.

Donors are primarily interested in knowing three things when you approach them for a gift. First, they want to know "what." What the gift will be used for within your organization is useful for the donor to know, but it's not what the donor is seeking here—even if that's what they say. The potential investor wants to know how this investment in you will fuel their vision, their goals.

For you to answer donors' queries effectively, you need to do some up-front research, whether it's particular to the individual donor in a face-to-face ask or a more general level of understanding based on demographics for a general appeal.

Second, a potential investor to your cause wants to know "when." "Yes, I know," you say, "I need to know when I'll receive the funds. How will it be paid out?" These issues aren't irrelevant to the donor but here again, it's not what's primarily on the donor's mind.

The "when" for the donor is how this request fits into his or her own life situation. The Germans even have a term for it: sitz im leiben. *It's more than simply where they are in their careers, whether they have children at home, whether there has been a divorce, death, or other significant life event. The situation of which I am speaking is their existential situation. It's their fundamental understanding of life's meaning and where they're going.*

Why is this even important? Because philanthropy is inextricably tied to a donor's spiritual state. It is part and parcel with how they perceive themselves and how they see themselves fitting into the larger universe.

The donor's situation in life is linked to their relationship with your organization. How long has the donor been involved with your cause? What levels of commitment have been made before this event?

Lastly, donors want to know "why." If you've done your homework and there is true affinity between the prospective investor and the societal improvement you want to make, then you're halfway there. The "why" question isn't about the case you're making. It's about your organization. Why should the investor choose to make this investment in you as opposed to another organization with a similar societal goal?

To answer this, you'll need to know the values that are important to the investor. Do they relate and truly align with those of your organization? The donor wants satisfaction of these values.

OK, so I'm sure you're thinking, "But this still doesn't tell me how much to ask for."

Although consideration of these variables doesn't tell you "how much," it defines your boundaries and points you toward "the number."

To illustrate how this works in real life, allow me to relate a personal donor experience.

Bill was well known to the organization I was representing. Although a generous man, his cumulative giving over a period of several years represented only a fraction of his true financial capacity.

There were many reasons for Bill's apparent lack of what a fundraiser might call capacity giving. What's important, however, is how this particular ask came to be. Bill gave me the outstanding opening of telling me in advance what his interest was. Not every donor will do this so openly. Regardless, with a bit of research and detective work, you can arrive at an accurate understanding.

Bill's interest was larger, more strategic, and certainly costlier than any of his previous gifts. When we put the gift proposal before Bill, he carefully reviewed how we planned to make his dream a reality. As Bill reviewed our proposal, he was impressed with our thoughtfulness and professionalism. His dream was in good hands with us. We would make good on it.

The price was very much the afterthought. Bill just wanted to check that we were asking for enough to get the job done. Again, a sign of professionalism.

Bill's sitz im leiben *was perfectly aligned with our own organizational needs. His transformational investment would have never happened without this alignment.*

How much? Frame your request in terms of an outcome aligned with the donor's values and the dollar amount becomes a no-brainer. What's more—the donor will think so as well.

Do the hard work and put yourself in the mind of your prospective investor. Feel what they are feeling. See what they are seeing.

There is inevitably a moment of truth—the request for support and the subsequent answer—not to be feared, over deliberated, or given merely a casual thought, but embraced as an opportunity for transformation. That's true for both you and the giver.

Chances are, you'll hit the bull's-eye every time.

• • •

Larry's story about Bill is a wonderful example of how to think about prospective donors from their point of view and to utilize the solicitation process to a successful outcome. That is a great way to determine the right amount to request from a donor.

CHAPTER 21

The Solicitation Environment

So far, I have been challenging you to become a better fundraiser. Now let's talk about getting comfortable. Believe it or not, that can be a challenge as well.

It is incredibly important to create the right environment when you make a solicitation call with a donor. You want them to feel comfortable. And you need to feel comfortable as well so that you can be confident and prepared to lead the meeting that is about to unfold.

Let's start first with the venue: the more private the better. I'm not a fan of restaurants for solicitation calls, unless they're very private or you can meet in a private room. You could also meet at the donor's office if you know from experience that the donor won't be interrupted. A home visit can work as well if you've been there before and have a sense of the dynamics about the home.

A meeting can quickly go sideways in the wrong environment, as a recent experience that I had with a donor will attest. I had had a series of meetings with this donor over many years. We had a wonderful relationship, and we were set to have a significant gift discussion. The donor suggested that we meet at a private club for breakfast. I had been there before to conduct previous solicitations. I knew the environment, I knew the staff, and I knew it could work. Breakfast tends to draw a sparse crowd, ensuring privacy. In fact, I asked my assistant to call ahead and have the club reserve a table in the farthest corner where we were sure not to be disturbed.

My plan was to get there early, as I usually do, have that first cup of coffee, and gather my thoughts. I wanted to tell one of the staff that once I pulled out my iPad and put it on the table for a presentation, no one should come up and offer us coffee or clear the table. We should be left alone.

That morning I arrived fifteen minutes early for an 8 a.m. meeting. As I walked into the room, I discovered that the donor was already there. And he wasn't sitting at the table I had designated. It was awkward.

I said to the staff member, "Look, that table's not going to work for us. It's in the middle of the room. We need something very private," and I pointed to the far end of the room. The staff member responded, "It's already reserved."

I didn't have the presence of mind to realize it was reserved for me. I settled for an alternate table she had identified.

I walked over to greet the donor and asked, "Do you mind? I'd like something a little more private?"

"Oh, sure. That would be fine, Martin."

We followed the staff member to another table. As she pulled out a chair, I thought, "That's the perfect chair for the donor." But the donor said, "Martin, why don't you take that chair." He proceeded to sit at the other chair and I thought, okay, I'll take the one offered to me. But it really wasn't the chair I wanted. This was going to be a very big discussion. I was presenting some important ideas: two $5 million options and a $10 million option, all naming opportunities for a capital construction project. I wanted to use the iPad to go through a series of illustrations and to focus on these three opportunities with the donor. However, because of how we were seated, I was going to have to use my iPad with my left hand. I'm right-handed. This arrangement required me to be less comfortable for that very important part of the conversation.

Despite my concerns, I was able to successfully work the iPad with my left hand. And the donor did not say no. In fact, he said he would give serious consideration to our discussion. I left quite hopeful that this would result in some very good news.

Today I chuckle about that visit, but I learned from it, to be sure. Creating the right environment is so very important. Planning for it, getting the lay of the land, and getting there early all play a role in a successful outcome.

It's also important to adapt to the situation when it is not ideal. Say you did all of the planning I have advised but still you were put at a disadvantage. Don't let it derail your presentation. Take a deep breath and work with what has been presented to you.

Another fundraiser with some wisdom to share is Orv Kimbrough. Orv has been president and CEO of the United Way of Greater St. Louis since 2013. His agency is one of the top five United Way affiliates in the nation, and it raises over $75 million annually. Orv started with United Way in 2007 as vice president of major gifts.

• • •

Martin's point of view is what I call a proverbial mic drop: he's covered all of the basics to create the conditions for making a successful major gift ask. There is nothing that I disagree with. Environment and context make all the difference in the world in securing any gift.

As Martin suggests, I believe the best way to solicit a major gift is face-to-face. This can also be the most stressful, uncomfortable, and labor-intensive way to request support. In my experience, nearly half of the investors that I ask face-to-face say yes to my request. Early in my United Way career, I learned something significant watching my boss navigate major gift meetings. Creating the right environment also includes watching what you eat. I rarely saw him eat anything other than tomato soup. I observed this for the first ten meetings. As he ordered soup, I would order a double cheeseburger with fries—every time! I figured initially that he was being health conscious, while I ate well.

One day I asked him what was up with the soup. He said, "I learned as a young staffer that when I was out meeting with donors, they were generally concerned at the fact that I ordered food but didn't eat during the meeting." I was somewhat shocked by this discovery: people are watching what I eat. He continued, "When you order soup, no one can tell how much you are eating and you can keep the conversation focused on the discussion at hand."

Another way to ask for a major gift is through a personal phone call. While not optimal, sometimes this cannot be avoided, as I often work with busy people who travel extensively. I have had conversations that have closed gifts from $10,000 to $300,000 and find that, as you might expect, the higher the amount of the request, the more likely the closing will happen in person. My conversion rate for new major gifts via phone is lower than the face-to-face asks.

Personal letters are a low-barrier way to ask prospects and returning investors for gifts. This has been my least effective solicitation method. Although you can get a reasonable response rate from a letter request if the individual has a relationship with you or your organization, most letters lack the ability to connect deeply. Don't stop with a personal letter.

I have always believed that the best way to engage any individual donor is face-to-face. But, in the United Way context and description of major gifts, I had a larger challenge. I had too many donors to effectively engage person-

ally. I needed a plan to create the conditions that would lead each investor to give, and to give more. I started out by redefining what we meant by major gifts. Major gifts as a concept for our organization became any gift greater than $10,000 while our leadership giving became any gift of $1,000 or more.

Now that I had a way to think about our major gift investors, I needed to create the right environment that would encourage them to give. When you aggregate givers around their similarities, the result is major giving groups, or affinities. We worked hard to expand the existing affinity groups: an African American giving group, a women's giving group, and a group of givers who donated $10,000 or more to United Way.

Using this model, we tried to create other meaningful communities, while striving to be as inclusive of our larger donor base as possible. We decided to create a young giving group, a multicultural group, and a small business group. A couple of years later, we created a retiree group, a men's group, and even smaller committees within existing affinities.

The theory was if we could get people of common interests, origins, or outlooks in the same space to talk about their aspirations for our community and about United Way's mission and work, we would create the right environment for continued and increased giving. We hosted these groups at interesting places, like a newly opened restaurant, and connected attendees to well-known or highly respected individuals they wouldn't ordinarily engage with. We saw that it was impossible for staff to personally visit with six-thousand-plus donors, so we had to create different types of relationships. We leveraged groups of volunteers, who themselves had circles that they influenced. We leveraged corporations and seeded our affinity groups within a corporate context; corporations call these employee resource groups.

Because we had so many people that we needed to reach, learn from, and engage, we tried a number of tactics. In addition to creating these communities within corporations, we knew that we needed to try to sit down with more of our donors giving at the $10,000 level and above. So, we did that. I worked with our then-CEO to visit with twenty-five to fifty of these donors each year. These meetings generally took place in a restaurant. The purpose of these initial meetings was to say thank you and build a better relationship by understanding their interests. Generally, we would bring collateral and marketing materials to help make the point about their investments. But mostly, we listened.

Our efforts worked! Over several years, leadership giving and major gifts both grew significantly. This group outpaced all other giving at our United Way.

• • •

Orv's commentary underscores the importance of having the right environment for a solicitation call. Further, he reinforces other areas that we have focused upon in the book—establishing floors, managing relationships, and developing ways to provide personal attention to higher-level donors.

CHAPTER 22

The Triple Play

Baseball provides us with a whole host of metaphors that we can apply to our lives. There's a shutout, a home run, and—my favorite for fundraising—the triple play.

In my world as a fundraiser, the triple play amounts to:

- Annual support
- Special support
- Deferred giving

Often when I call on a donor, I do not ask for money that day. I am there to lay the groundwork for future giving. So, I will say to the donors, "Mark and Lynda, it's so great to be with you today. One of the things I want to talk with you about is the kind of giving our alumni do on behalf of the university. There are three ways our alumni support the university, and there are three ways that, over the course of time, we would like you to participate as well." Then I outline the three types of support our institution relies on.

First there is annual support. Annual contributions provide us with critically needed funds. They allow us to address contemporaneous needs and challenges and, by so doing, enable us to pursue excellence. Annual support for the university comes largely from our alumni and their generosity. These gifts come to us in various sizes, from a few dollars to many thousands of dollars. The common denominator is that they come annually (though some people have established monthly payment plans). These gifts are a recognition by the donors that they are taking responsibility for buttressing the work of our university. In many cases, donors direct that money to a unique aspect of the campus. We offer these annual donors membership in our Pierre Laclede Society, which recognizes those who support the university annually at $1,000 or more. The program has grown to more than 1,880 donors and most are alumni.

The second part of the triple play comprises special gifts. These can be in the form of endowed scholarships, gifts for buildings, programming, establishing professorships, and chairs. Oftentimes these come to us because of the particular interests of donors, and we help dovetail those interests with the needs of the university.

Finally, there is the deferred gift, which can become an ultimate gift from a donor. Typically, these are the largest gifts some people make, often coinciding with their death. They might come in the form of a bequest or proceeds from an insurance policy. We have advisors on staff who are available to work with our alumni to provide counsel about these types of gifts.

So that's the triple play. Once I introduce the concept in an initial call, I can refer to it in subsequent visits. That makes it easy for me (and here comes another baseball metaphor) to make my pitch.

Ellen Howe, managing director for the Rome Group, a St. Louis-based consulting firm to nonprofits and former vice president of financial development at the then YMCA of Greater St. Louis, offers more thoughts on the triple play.

• • •

Although promoting annual gifts, special gifts, and deferred gifts is good for our organization, I believe that it is also good for our donors. Over the past fifteen years, we have seen more emphasis on donor-centered fundraising. Quite simply, it is not just about getting donors to support our institution; it is about developing a respectful relationship with our donors.

Martin writes about laying the groundwork for the three ways in which alumni can support his institution early in their relationship. This is wise of Martin, but many fundraisers do not have this opportunity. Because of the demands of their organization, I have seen development professionals focus all their attention on completing the annual fund drive or the capital campaign. Unless deferred gifts are included in the capital campaign or heavily promoted by the nonprofit, many development professionals only educate donors about planned-giving opportunities when their time allows. That means they rarely, if ever, talk about planned giving.

So how as fundraisers do we complete the triple play? We do this by keeping our focus on the donors. In developing a meaningful relationship with our donors, we gain an understanding of their values, their interests in our institution, and their circumstances. With this information, we educate our donors about the many ways in which they can support our organization, thus allowing our donors the flexibility to make gifts in ways that fit within their financial means and make the desired impact.

In addition to educating our donors, we also need to invite them to consider a special gift or a planned gift. I will use myself as an example. When I was working at the YMCA and was promoted, Chris, my previous boss, called and asked me to become a member of the Lamplighter Society, the Y's legacy group. I started laughing because I never considered myself someone with the resources to make a planned gift or significant gift. Chris first said that he knew how important the Y's camp program was to me, and he thought I would like to make a lasting gift. Chris had me with those comments. All we had to do was figure out a planned-giving vehicle that would work for me. Chris facilitated the next step, which was a meeting with a financial advisor to discuss a life insurance policy. Because Chris knew my interests, asked for my gift, and educated me on how I could make a significant planned gift, I became a proud member of the YMCA's Lamplighter Society.

It really is that simple. Develop a relationship with your donors, educate them about the ways in which they can support your institution, and then ask for their gift.

• • •

Ellen makes some very important points here. What is particularly striking about her story about Chris is how he touched her heart. Ellen likely would not have considered a planned gift at that time, but he reminded her of the meaning that the camp had for her and he offered membership as part of the recognition and support for her generosity. He also showed her that what seemed impossible really wasn't. That made all the difference. Chris acted as a thoughtful and well-prepared executive director when he reached out to Ellen when and as he did.

CHAPTER 23

The Preemptive Strike

In the previous chapter, we used a baseball metaphor: the triple play. Now let's talk about something that can happen before you can even make your pitch. I call it the preemptive strike. (I know I am mixing my metaphors here, moving from the ball field to the battlefield, but please bear with me.)

In terms of military action, a preemptive strike is designed to neutralize a potential threat or to gain an advantage over an enemy. I'm not suggesting that donors and prospective donors view us as enemies. We may be seen as a potential threat in some respects, however, as they may have many commitments, and what we may be asking of them will have ramifications in their lives. As a result, they will sometimes resort to their own preemptive strike.

The preemptive strike works something like this: The donor welcomes you. You're seated. They have gracious smiles on their faces. And they say, "We're so glad you're here. We've spent so much time talking about what a great organization you have since we saw that we had an appointment with you. And we respect it. We're proud to be associated with it. So, we thought we could save us all a lot of time and energy here. We have something for you."

They reach across and give you a check for $5,000.

Well, if you were there to ask for $1,000 or $2,500 or $5,000, hey, all right, fantastic. But if you're there to ask for $100,000 or $250,000, well, there's a little bit of a gap between the two!

I remember the first time this happened to me, nearly twenty years ago. The donor handed me a check for several thousand dollars. I was at his office, and I was completely flustered. I didn't know what to do. I thanked the donor and he was on his feet almost immediately.

I said, "I so appreciate this. It will be helpful. I'll tell the bishop and there are some other things we hope to talk to you about in the future." And I kind of mumbled, stumbled, and fumbled my way out the door holding a check for a few thousand dollars but not having accomplished anywhere near what I had set out to do for the visit that day.

Now I've learned to handle this differently. The donor presents a check for $5,000. I look at it and I'm appreciative. "Thank you so much for this $5,000. What a terrific gift, an indication, as you've said, of your interest and commitment to our organization."

Then I take that check and put it down between the donor and me. I say, "But you know, since we have this appointment, I would like to take a few minutes to tell you about the project for which we've come to have this conversation and some of the good news already associated with this undertaking. Would you mind if I took a few minutes to do so?"

Presuming the donor says yes, I am on my way to success. I present the case exactly as I intended to and talk about the success we have had to date, highlighting those donors who have given equivalent sums of money to what I intended to ask of these donors. Better yet, if they are peers of this donor, and if the donor knows these people, and they are equivalent in the civic community, then this can be additionally helpful in the conversation. I can say, "What I was hoping to do is have a discussion with you today about a commitment of $250,000, as John and Jane have supported, and Mike and Angela have supported. Would you join them? I know you know them. Would you make a similar commitment to help us meet this incredibly important objective?"

I might get the response, "We can't do that. Five thousand dollars is what we're prepared to do today."

I will then say, "Well, suppose we were able to create more time for this. Maybe several years—three, four, even five years. If you had up to five years to fulfill this kind of commitment, would you give it serious consideration? In fact, we could discuss using a deferred gift vehicle, too. Like a charitable gift annuity that actually provides for you a stream of income for the remainder of your life." And you go from there. Rather than allowing the conversation to be preempted by this generous donor, you press on exactly as you had planned.

You make the ask. You do the best you can. And then what happens, happens. But you haven't let this $5,000 stand in the way of what you prepared and planned to do.

A former colleague of mine and currently vice president for university advancement at Bradley University, Jacob Heuser has developed an outstanding track record as a fundraiser over the past decade. He, too, has experience with the preemptive strike.

• • •

Martin is right on the money when he talks about the preemptive strike. One way to deal with it is to understand your donors and where they are coming from. We deal with a lot of smart, sophisticated people who have a lot of wealth, but that doesn't mean they understand philanthropy and how it might apply to your organization.

Donors don't always understand what it might cost to make a real impact in your setting. They may, for instance, think in terms of scholarships. We love scholarships. They are impactful for so many students. But now, the university may have other pressing needs.

It really helps when starting this conversation—and in avoiding the preemptive strike—to have built a relationship with the donor. It's important to do a lot of listening before you do the asking. What is it that the donor wants to accom-

plish through their philanthropy? How can a donation be meaningful both to that family and to the university?

I remember speaking with one couple that was thinking about supporting some scholarships. This would have been nice, but we were thinking bigger. We were hoping to fund a building addition. Sometimes bricks and mortar aren't as meaningful to donors who are thinking about students. But you can make it personal by showing them how state-of-the-art facilities help students achieve mastery in their fields and lead successful lives and, in fact, create legacies of their own for the next generation.

With this couple, I asked if I could bring back a proposal to create a learning space in our health science building.

I could tell discussing money wasn't comfortable for them. They had been thinking they were just going to provide some money for a student. But I was able to talk about how they could affect the lives of hundreds of students with their donation. The wife in this instance had worked in the field, so she could appreciate what the facility could mean. She also knew that many of her fellow students did not go on to make a whole lot of money. Understanding and appreciating this, I was able to say, "We don't know a whole lot of people in the field who can support us with a donation for a capital improvement like this."

And they both responded most generously. We talked about how to set up the donation in a way that made it easy and most affordable for them. And in that way, we went from what had been a donation for scholarships in the thousands of dollars to a six-figure donation that including putting their names on that learning space.

• • •

The preemptive strike can cause new fundraisers to stumble, but remembering your purpose will see you through. When you relate that purpose to donors and show them what their contributions could mean for others, they are much more likely to step up and deliver what you have asked for.

CHAPTER 24

Leadership from the Front

"Leadership from the front" is a theme that I have been presenting to donors at our university for many years. The idea is that every human being is called to be a leader—to take what talents and abilities they have and use them to improve the world. All of us are called to be leaders.

In the organizations in which we operate, there isn't one leader. We are all leaders. But, among leaders, some lead from the front. Often these leaders are those who are most senior in our organizations. They are those with foresight and vision. In many cases, they have created organizations. They have taken great risks, sometimes failed, and have learned from those experiences. They bring sharp business acumen to bear on these organizations.

At our university, there are a few such people who have served as leaders from the front through volunteering, insightful counsel, and tremendous philanthropy.

I bring up the idea of leadership from the front in my solicitation calls. I talk to donors about how they have been leaders from the front in their organizations, in the community, and on our behalf, and how vital that leadership has been for our university. Then I will say, "Max and Karen, I'd like you to consider stepping forward once more to be leaders from the front for our university." I will tell them what I have in mind: the nature of the gift, a need that we have, or an opportunity that we have that invites them to step forward.

I have found that this concept resonates deeply with these leaders. When they hear this description of leadership, they think to themselves, "Yes, that's me." It captures their self-identity, what they've made of themselves over time, and how they're functioning today in the world. To be a leader from the front requires terrific energy, commitment, dedication, skill, and ability. When we affirm that they are leaders from the front, it emphasizes their dignity, their self-understanding, and their years of determination and hard work. And when we tie it all back to the university, they want to be helpful. They want to meet the request, if possible, or think with us about how to get others to join with them to address the opportunities we have presented.

Leadership from the front is a very powerful theme. I encourage you to consider how to use it with outstanding donors with whom you have the privilege of working as you facilitate their philanthropy for your organization.

I shared my thoughts on this concept with Joan Nesbitt, vice chancellor for university advancement at Missouri University of Science and Technology in Rolla, Missouri, and asked her to add her own. Joan looks at leadership as a responsibility that we all must undertake and challenge one another to exercise.

• • •

Google the word leadership *and you can find as many definitions and models as you can find leadership gurus. There's no shortage of folks peddling ideas and assertions about this most crucial aspect of our fundraising enterprise. But the definition I most appreciate, which was presented to me at a leadership conference sponsored by the University of Chicago Booth School of Business, is this one: "Leadership is taking responsibility for the influence you have in the world."*

How about that? It's short and there's no strategic-this or vision-that, no business jargon to cloud this definition's simple but powerful essence. Leadership is taking responsibility for your influence.

And what about influence? We all have it. And we all use it. At the risk of sounding like a crank, not everybody uses it for good. And it seems as if fewer and fewer so-called leaders take responsibility for the impact of their influence. That's why I like this notion of responsible-influence-as-leadership so much.

Professional fundraisers who take responsibility for their influence understand that we answer to more than the university president. We answer to our academic colleagues, who work with us to create and promote philanthropic opportunities with win-win outcomes for our students and charitable partners. We answer to our donors, who give generously of their wealth and who take us at our word. We answer to each other, especially as young staff turn to more seasoned fundraisers for assistance when the work gets tricky in matters of interpersonal relationships, ethics, politics, and more. We answer to society at large as we seek to uphold the ideals attendant to higher education, notably wisdom, mastery, and integrity.

But influence works on both sides of the fundraising equation. Every fundraiser I know has encountered at least one donor who seeks outsized influence in exchange for his or her donation. A purely quid pro quo exchange, especially when unspoken, can be alluring to ambitious fundraisers and donors alike. However, using our influence responsibly demands that we not merely conduct ourselves honorably, but that we inspire our donors to the highest aims of charity, a word which—in its origins—is akin to cherish *and is rooted in love.*

If we cherish each other and the organization that binds us, there is no path forward except one that weds influence with responsibility. Together, they are like flint to steel and enkindle leadership that serves us all.

• • •

As Joan describes, leadership cuts both ways. We must be the very best we can be, just as we call upon our donors to so act on the behalf of our organizations.

CHAPTER 25

Saving the Best for Last

Take a few moments to consider an idea. I call it "saving the best for last." When we engage donors or prospective donors, it can be most effective to save the solicitation for later in the call.

When I make a call to discuss a possible donation, I first think about how it should be structured. I like to use what occurs early in the conversation to build up to the request. After establishing rapport and as we settle into the visit, I will summarize why I'm there.

I'll say, "Mary, I appreciate you taking the time to visit with me today. And there are several things I'd like us to talk about. I'd like to talk about your volunteer service at the university and how that has been going. I want to talk about a challenge at the university that I know will be of concern to you and get your thoughts about it. And then I'd like to talk about your philanthropy."

I will approach those topics in the order presented. When I use that phrase "your philanthropy," it triggers a dynamic. Mary begins thinking something like, "Oh, Martin is here to talk about my philanthropy. Is he here to talk about a gift from me? How much? Will I be able to say yes? Will I want to say yes? I don't want to disappoint Martin, but I may have to. I have many considerations."

That phrase builds anticipation, fear, and sometimes discomfort. It gets the donor thinking about what matters most in our call: their next round of support for our institution.

Sometimes tension is a good thing. It can prepare the donor to be alert, focused, and wide awake, listening to every word when we finally get to saying what we've saved for last.

In this call structuring, I will also introduce commentary early to help reinforce a theme of leadership. Often, I'll give them a fundraising update about the institution and mention whether some peers of theirs have recently given additional support or graduated to a new milestone in their cumulative giving. I may also talk about an individual and the size and nature of that person's gift. Again, this is a set-up of what I'll ask from the donor later in the call. And then, eventually, I will get us there.

Sometimes donors don't want to wait. They want to let me know something, like the fact that they may not be able to make any gift at this point. Or they may well introduce philanthropy just so they can deal with it quickly and release the tension they feel. Sometimes that's fine. But more often I believe I need to provide additional information to make my case. So, I will continue my course after acknowledging their comments.

I was recently at a brunch with a donor and a fellow fundraiser when the donor interrupted our carefully structured conversation to deal with the gift. I said to the donor, "I appreciate your sharing that with us," and then I went right back to what I wanted to lay out for the donor. In doing so, while the tension remained, I was able to put in place a context for a more fully informed discussion and for what we wanted the donor to consider.

By saving the best for last, by creating a context for donors and providing the best possible reasons for them to make a charitable contribution, we increase the satisfaction they will experience through making a gift that will enrich and ennoble their lives.

My friend John Sentovich, formerly chief development officer for the Northern Illinois University Foundation, has a story that provides a different take on "best for last"—as in leaving a legacy.

• • •

The year was 2008 and the stock market was in the throes of the Great Recession. The timing of the crash could not have been worse, as many of us in major and planned-gift fundraising rely on gifts of appreciated securities to help our organizations fulfill their noble missions. Oh, and they are important in helping us hit our fundraising goals! With the market tumbling, some at my university wondered if we would see any gifts like these in the foreseeable future.

Our spirits as fundraisers were down, to say the least. I was wondering if it was time for a career change.

I had been at the university less than a year, implementing a new planned giving program. I knew that the market would eventually correct itself and that gifts of stock would rebound as well, so I committed to double down my efforts with our planned gift marketing plan. The centerpiece of our plan was a newsletter called "Cornerstone," which also was the name of our planned giving society. Every issue had a call to action that consisted of a series of checkboxes to request more information about an article, or a brochure on a planned giving topic, or a request to be enrolled in the Cornerstone Society as the donor had already remembered our university in his or her estate plan.

Our planned giving team put great effort into each issue and considered every detail. Are the articles compelling enough? Are they the right length? Will the student and donor stories move people to respond? Do the pictures draw people in? Are we mailing to the right people? With the help of our consultant, the program was producing the kind of results we had hoped and the responses to each issue were growing. This was important because our marketing is what produced leads for us, which led to appointments, which led to solicitations and eventually gifts. At first, most of our planned gifts were bequests in the $25,000–$50,000 range, but as I got to know our donors, I knew larger gifts were possible if we stayed focused and worked the plan. We also marketed charitable gift annuities regularly.

In the second year of the program, we received a reply card that seemed rather innocuous, but it differed from most as it was returned not by the donor, but by the donor's CPA. The card said the donor would like to discuss with a representative from our university including the College of Business in his estate plan. It also said he had cancer and wanted to get something done as soon as possible. The school would likely get his entire estate. Clearly, they got our attention.

A wise colleague of mine once said that fundraising is akin to fishing, and that the more lines you have in the water, the better the chances you have of catching something. He also said that occasionally a fisherman, once he knows he has a big one on the line, will drop everything to reel it in. Something told me I had to drop everything.

Soon I was on my way to northern Wisconsin to find out who this donor was and what type of legacy he was considering. We spent the first meeting getting to know one another, listening to what he was hoping to accomplish with his gift, and why his alma mater changed his life.

If you look up "millionaire next door" in the dictionary, you will see his picture. He was unassuming, humble, shy, and a bit standoffish. There was not one symbol of wealth or excess in his very modest ranch home and I wondered if the trip would bear any meaningful fruit. But I figured since I had made the six-hour trip to meet him, I should listen closely for donative intent. Turns out he had it in spades. He graduated from our accountancy department in the sixties, worked as a data analyst for an oil company for thirty years, and retired to northern Wisconsin to live near his father, who, as fate would have it, died six months after he moved north. Several minutes into our conversation I also learned that he was an NMNK donor: never married, no kids. Things continued to get interesting.

As I listened, I learned that his alma mater gave him all that he had: his terrific career, access to wealth he never thought possible, and the ability to enjoy a rare coin collection that would be the envy of his friends and neighbors. I learned, too, that he wanted to do something that had never been done in the College of Business.

Our next meeting was in a month to go over the paperwork for the first-ever professorship in the Department of Accountancy. He also decided to fund the largest universitywide scholarship endowment. It would provide students financial aid so that their degrees would launch their careers mostly debt-free. I could tell his philanthropy was providing the kind of energy and enthusiasm he hoped it would as he neared the home stretch of his life.

A final visit was with the chair of the Department of Accountancy, which gave him a face for his gift. This visit further solidified his decision to be philanthropic, as the chair was experienced, wise, and thoughtful and could answer all his questions with the precision they demanded.

Some six months after that visit, I learned that his cancer had taken a turn for the worse, so we waited.

When I learned my donor had passed, I discovered that like most accountants, he had his affairs in good order. The estate settled quickly, and my university received the largest gift that year: $1.5 million. There were several takeaways from this gift: Don't worry about what the stock market is doing; you can't control that. Control the things you can control, like producing quality mailings, making time to set up donor visits, and listening for cues about the legacy a donor wants to leave your institution.

Leaving a legacy—that truly is saving the best for last.

• • •

The way John worked with this donor very much underscores the deliberate and thoughtful way that a fundraiser can engage donors to perform a magnificent act of generosity in their last days. While we thoughtfully structure our calls to lead to a desirable outcome, far more profoundly, donors structure their lives and their philanthropy, oftentimes saving their best for last.

EPILOGUE

As I stated in the Introduction, *Five Minutes for Fundraising: A Collection of Expert Advice from Gifted Fundraisers* is a book to focus on you, to help you find your purpose in fundraising, be of service to others, and help transform our world for the better. Whatever your reason for picking this book up and reading it, I hope the time you spent has been worthwhile.

Your interest in fundraising is inspired likely by an organization that you care deeply about and requires additional resources to fulfill its mission. I hope that this book instructed you about asking for resources with respect for donors and instilled you with confidence as you apply the approaches and techniques that have been described. My hope is that now, you will go forth and exercise the will and courage to ask people to invest in the organizations that you believe are worthy of support. Asking for money for outstanding organizations is honorable, invaluable, even priceless work.

AFTERWORD

Why Do People Give?

by Fred Alvis Bleeke

As we have heard many times, Americans are very generous people.

What is it in our way of life that "helps us" to donate money? What is it in American history, polity, and culture that significantly supports philanthropy?

The key question is, why do people give?

You may be surprised to discover where we find the fertile soil that bears our answer.

But first, the following story—an admiration for all past and present students stumped on exam questions—may set the stage for an investigation into the question, why?

A student, let us call him Jay, was taking his final exam in physics. It was only one question, asking "why does such and such a reaction take place" on some esoteric subject that apparently had never come up in class. All the students were stunned, but most began writing lengthy answers anyway. Jay started to write, but nothing much came to mind. He put his pencil down and handed in his paper.

Upon returning to class to receive the results of his exam, he was surprised to see that he had made an A-plus while all the other students were feeling dejected about their grades. Across the top of Jay's exam paper the professor had scribbled "Excellent!" Jay had written just one word: "Because." Nothing had come to his mind to follow. So, to the professor's question "Why?" the student's response was, "Because."

Why do people give? The answer could be "Because."

"Because we were asked" may be the most regular response when we question donors why they gave. But, why (if that is truly why they gave) did the donors respond favorably to the request for money? "Because of who is asking" is a possible explanation.

Other donor responses are "Because we want to" and "Because it feels good." Let's see what lies underneath these donor statements. In so doing, we will find motivations for giving that are brought to the surface and can be revealing for us as we engage in philanthropy.

There are three key constitutional rights in the United States that have distinctively shaped philanthropy. Yes, rights and freedoms guaranteed in the Constitution of the United States support us in our giving and receiving. That can be surprising to many of us. It is almost as if this treasure for the understanding of philanthropy is hidden in plain sight.

The reasons that donors give—the expressions that affect their decision making—most often fall into one of the following broad categories:

- Instruction expression: Taught to give
- Spiritual/sharing expression: Blessed/benefited in giving
- Association expression: Desire to join others
- Identity expression: Fulfillment of self-identity and who we think others think we are
- Exchange expression: Give to get
- Perpetuation expression: Extending values and beliefs forward in time and place.

Generosity is universal. It is not just an American trait. However, we have freedoms, incentives, and institutional structures that allow philanthropy to thrive.

Giving Flows from Rich Deposits

"Congress shall make no law respecting an establishment of religion, or prohibiting the free exercise thereof."

An unlikely place to look for an answer to the question, Why do we give?, is expressed in the First Amendment to the United States Constitution, our freedom of religion.

Religions provide lessons on how we should live. Sometimes the lessons are inspirational and sometimes they serve as commandments; and, therein, we can see that people give because they are taught to give.

If we want to find the early traces of philanthropy in the United States, we can look to the sacred writings the pioneers carried with them. It is easy to leap to the Puritans or our religious forebears as consumers of these holy words.

However, generosity for the public good did not begin with monotheistic inspiration. The Roman and even Greek empires had noted patrons and philanthropists building theaters, places of worship, public baths, and even more infrastructure items like roads, bridges, and water systems.

Also, think about the Native Americans and their early spirit of generosity to the European "visitors." If it were not for the people who were already here sharing with the newly arrived white people during that first winter and succeeding years, most of the immigrants would not have survived.

What about the early Christian settlers in America?

On the way over to Colonial America in 1630, the future first governor of Massachusetts, the Puritan John Winthrop, delivered a sermon titled "A Model of Christian Charity" wherein he stated that God counts himself "more honored in dispensing his gifts to man by man than if He did it by His own immediate hand." Reread that. It says God is *more honored* when a person makes a gift to another than if God provides the gift.

Reverend Winthrop's motivational instruction was that people have needs for others and they must be knit into a giving community if they were to survive and flourish. The right way of living was for them to be givers together. People were being taught to give.

One of the great preachers in the Colonial period was Cotton Mather. His most popular item was a tract titled "Essays to Do Good." Mather urged neighbors forward with "a perpetual endeavor to do good in the world." While he saw giving as individualistic and voluntary, his genius—in an American sense—was his urgings to gather people together to meet the needs of others.

Injunctions like those from the sermons of Winthrop, Mather, and many other preachers were clearly teaching people to give. And it's true today. Sermons by clergy are providing rich deposits that can be tapped for the public good. While "storing up treasures in heaven," people are motivated to invest in ways pleasing to God in the here and now.

Following are two brief examples of what is being taught. A Jewish injunction from Proverbs 3:9–10: "Honor the Lord with your wealth and with the first and best part of all your income. Then your barns will be full, and your vats will overflow with fresh wine."

Meanwhile, the physician turned historian, Luke, writes, "Give, and you will receive. A large quantity, pressed together, shaken down, and running over will be put into your pocket" (God's Word Bible, Luke 6:38a).

Many more sacred writings are taught and practiced. Philanthropy is thereby expanded.

Brian O'Connell, in *America's Voluntary Spirit,* leads off with the quote, "A very large part of America's attractive voluntary spirit stems from our religious heritage." Doug Lawson in his 1991 book, *Give to Live,* writes, "A religious or spiritual connection is clearly the driving force behind much of American's benevolence."

What other lessons are learned from benevolence? People tell us how they are spiritually blessed in their giving. They say they grow in their faith. The rewards for them come in spiritual ways, such as finding needed comfort; extending new acts of kindness, love, and sharing; and, most often, the act of returning blessings they have received.

Let us now examine some research that shows that giving has physical benefits as well as spiritual blessings. In *Give to Live,* Lawson reports, "A ten-year study of the physical health and social activities of 2,700 men in Tecumseh, Michigan, found that those who did regular volunteer work had death rates two and one-half times lower than those who didn't."

Another study by two Harvard medical doctors, David McClelland and Carol Hirshnet, discovered that people who watched a documentary about Mother Teresa's work with the dying showed an increase in immunoglobin-A, the body's first line of defense again viral infection. When people watched other movies that didn't focus on compassion, there was no increase in immunoglobin-A.

The research findings of Professor Russell James at Texas Tech University records, "Charitable giving is rewarding ... [and] uniquely involves oxytocin-rich social attachment brain regions." Oxytocin is a hormone whose role in love is profound. James says, " ... increase it, increase giving."

The great American poet and philosopher Ralph Waldo Emerson explains: "It is one of the beautiful compensations of this life that no one can sincerely try to help another without helping himself."

Giving as Contributing Members in Community

"Congress shall make no law ... prohibiting ... the right of the people peaceably to assemble ... "

The second freedom key to philanthropy in the United States is the right to assemble. This right, together with the freedom of religion, is guaranteed in the First Amendment. Within the freedom to assemble are two expressions impacting fundraising:

- People give because they want to join with others.
- People give because giving fulfills who they think they are, or who they think others think they are.

We will examine both.

First, we are social beings. A leading American figure who fostered voluntary assemblies of people for public good was Benjamin Franklin. He was the most secular philanthropist of the Colonial period. While in his youth, he was known to have made fun of preacher Cotton Mather, yet in his older age, he credited "Essays to Do Good" as important in developing his persona as a "doer of good."

Here are some of Franklin's philanthropic activities as noted by Robert Bremner in his article "Doing Good in the New World" found in *America's Voluntary Spirit*:

> Starting in 1727 with the Junto, a club for the mutual improvement of its members, and the library (1731) which was the Junto's first offshoot, Franklin proceeded to organize or assist in organizing a host of civic projects. He founded a volunteer fire company, developed schemes for paving, cleaning, and lighting the streets of Philadelphia, and sponsored a plan for policing the city. . . . He played a leading part in the establishment of both the Pennsylvania Hospital (1751) and the academy which became the University of Pennsylvania . . ."

Look at that list! Certainly, Benjamin Franklin was an organizing philanthropist dealing with key issues of his day.

Rosemary Cass and Gordon Manser in *America's Voluntary Spirit* emphasize,

> Voluntary groups sprang up for a variety of reasons: reaction to the admittedly inadequate governmental care of the poor, desire to aid special groups in the population, the effective propa-

> gandizing of the social reformers, and the desire of many religious groups to provide for the needs of their own within the doctrine and structure of their church.

Beginning in the twentieth century, "organized" philanthropy stepped up to new levels. Up to that time in the United States, newspapers told about leading benefactors. Citizens were engaged in providing support through collections, offerings, dues, and subscriptions. In the late 1800s and early 1900s, we see the formation of national federations to provide opportunities for increased engagement. Next came fundraising campaigns. And that is when fundraising took on a more professional cast, although not necessarily seen as healthy by all the public. The raising of money was criticized because it involved paid fundraising staff, rather than just volunteers. It became clear, however, that organized fundraising campaigns needed added expertise to bring people together strictly to raise money.

And that brings us to the second expression. These paid staff or paid consultants recognized that people give because giving fulfills who they think they are, or who they think others think they are.

Membership organizations, in recruitment drives, recognize that new members often fit the profile of the existing members. People tend to associate with people like themselves. We connect to people who think and generally believe what we do. With our identities tied to the identities of others, we give together to accomplish what we all agree to do.

Identity of self includes personal recognition, but that is at a very basic level. For identity, we want to see how the person presents self in society. Psychological and sociological studies can show us much in this identity expression. The core questions related to the presentation of self in society are:

- "Who am I?"
- "How do I see myself?"
- "How do others see me?"

Some of us may remember the old humorous illustration, "Mr. Klein stands up in the temple and announces, 'I, Sam Klein, of J & W Fabrics, 199 West 38th Street, purveyors of the finest wool fabrics, give one hundred dollars—anonymously!'"

How can we think about such a man without a smile on our faces? Certainly, seemingly generous—identifying self with business and his business being the best business—and how so humble he is—anonymous even!

Again, it is good to repeat the maxim, "People give because giving fulfills who they think they are, or who they think others think they are." When being asked for money, we often are provided avenues to give that help us individually and collectively fulfill our identities.

Giving Is Honored in Law

"No person shall . . . be deprived of life, liberty, or property, without due process of law; nor shall private property be taken for public use, without just compensation."

A third key freedom for American philanthropy is in private property and contracts. This right flows from the Fifth Amendment to the United States Constitution. People give because they want to get.

In *Wealth in Western Thought,* published in 1994, Paul G. Schervish writes:

> Around the time of the Puritans, the new economic and cultural dispensation of capitalism led to the emergence of a new doctrine of economic responsibility summarized in the activist ethics of stewardship. In this "world turned upside down," to borrow Christopher Hill's apt phrase, the cultural scripture of wealth became reoriented. Financial asceticism now became oriented toward the quality of engagement with money as an expression of production, whereas previously it focused on the quality of disengagement from money in undertakings of consumption or charity.

The clear point Hill, author of *The World Turned Upside Down: Radical Ideas during the English Revolution,* and Schervish came to understand is that we are not to cleanse ourselves from our lucre but wisely use money and do something with it. Times were "a-changing," weren't they? Money became more of a currency for action.

We now turn our attention to a brief recounting of our tax laws. It is necessary to do so because it will be helpful to further understand why people expect to get something for their giving.

Hard to believe, but it is true: the United States did not have an income tax until 1913. The Revenue Act of that year set aside certain organizations, such as religious, educational, and charitable agencies, to be exempt from paying taxes. Then in 1917 Congress enacted an income tax law that permitted individuals to deduct charitable contributions up to a certain percentage of taxable income. In 1935, when the Social Security Act was passed and heavier taxes were placed on corporations, Congress passed a law permitting corporations to deduct charitable contributions up to 5 percent of taxable income.

The tax code appears to be very beneficial to the giving of money. However, it is important also to remember that philanthropy was practiced long before there were tax allowances for giving for charitable and religious purposes. The chapter titled "The Power of Reciprocity" describes how we as recipients feel an obligation to give back with no consideration for tax savings. Reciprocity gives us a chance to rebalance our social relationships.

The second expression within this construct is the perpetuation expression: People give because they want to extend themselves (and their values and beliefs) forward in time and place.

The defining legal case for American philanthropy could be the Trustees of Dartmouth College case of 1819. In this case the State of New Hampshire passed legislation increasing its control over Dartmouth College by giving the state the authority to appoint the college's board of trustees and, furthermore, ordered the college to report annually to the governor and state legislature.

The old trustees did not like that. They sued and won. Their key argument was that donors had given their funds and estates to Dartmouth and those donations were private contracts with the trustees and the college that needed to be honored.

Peter Dobkin Hall, in his "Historical Perspectives on Nonprofit Organizations," the first chapter of *The Jossey-Bass Handbook of Nonprofit Leadership and Management,* states, "The Dartmouth College case fundamentally redefined the nature of the corporation, transforming it from a delegate of public power over which the State could exercise control, to a private contract protected from government interference."

Going right along, we see that further protection for charitable trusts came about in 1844. It was the Girard case that gave the right for individuals to create charitable trusts and for corporations to manage the trusts.

Private property and private contracts, to be safe from government consumption, certainly were important in those days and so to this day—probably even more now since we have greatly increased our incomes and assets.

We look to use our money, and we want to see that it gets used the way we want it used. Period. For this urge to have who-I-am and what-I-value continue beyond the limits of one's self and life, we need property and contracts to be honored. In the philanthropy of yesterday, of today, and for tomorrow, we see our drives for perpetuation in the forms of buildings, endowments, and missions to be carried on. American law permits and even promotes these legacies held for the public good; and, certainly, that benefits us all.

Giving Sprouts from Treasured Soil

At any one moment in time, each of us is aware of so much more than what we are thinking or what our senses detect.

For example, a man driving seventy miles per hour on the highway may focus on some part of his schedule for the day. Then, he finds himself further down the road not remembering all the things that elapsed over the past few minutes. Yet, when a car came into his lane, he reacted.

We sense and know so much more than what we consciously recall. Without thinking about the reasons for our inclinations and responses to give, we feel the urge to connect our lives with others. Through our examination of the freedoms guaranteed to us in the Constitution of the United States, we have been looking below the surface of "why people give" to better understand our charitable actions.

Recently a friend was asked for a major gift for a fundraising campaign. While interested, she was not sure she would make the commitment. Later that week, she went to a club meeting and listened to a presentation on how much good is all about us and the importance of making the right decisions. She called the campaign offices and told the director she had decided to provide the leadership gift.

What all went on in her mind as she concluded to accept the invitation to participate in the campaign?

Could it have been that she knew the importance of helping others? She had been taught that.

Could it have been that she saw herself as a caring person? Her identity was wrapped up in how she saw herself.

Could it have been she knew her gift would perpetuate what she so much believed in?

In our many activities, we have motivations for the care of ourselves and for the care of others. We often may need to bring to consciousness these hidden understandings so that we can focus on what we really want to do—whether for our own care or for the support of others.

The concept of philanthropy is expanding. Many of us still call the giving of money to organizations "charitable giving." More and more, though, we are hearing and reading the term "philanthropy."

Charitable giving was once almost entirely focused on benefits to people and the quality of life for them. Today, we are including care for all the living through humane societies, animal protection groups, and environmental initiatives. So, the definition of philanthropy has become more encompassing and, yet, more precise. From Latin, *philanthropy* was earlier translated as "love of mankind," then more politically correct as "love of humankind," now "love of the living."

Since giving is becoming more and more a part of our lives, it seems helpful to learn more about why we give—about the constitutional pillars for voluntary collective action in the United States.

And, so, we have recognized three key, constitutionally guaranteed rights that undergird motivational expressions significantly impacting philanthropy:

- Freedom of religion
- Freedom to assemble
- Rights of private property and contracts

When we realize the support for philanthropy within the three freedoms and six corresponding expressions summarized below, we deepen our understanding about where the enduring generosity of Americans comes from.

Why do people give? We give:

- Because we are taught to give.
- Because we are blessed/benefited in our giving.
- Because we want to join with others.
- Because giving fulfills who we think we are, or who we think others think we are.

- Because we want to get.
- Because we want to extend ourselves (and our values and beliefs) forward in time and place.

By recognizing the freedoms we have and the reasons for American generosity, we grasp even more our own philanthropic motivations, adding greater meaning to our lives, our actions, our communities, and our legacy.

Finally, as Jim Lord, the creator of the Philanthropic Quest, so powerfully demonstrates at his workshops, "We will discover our own motivations when we see ourselves as we are—contributing members of society in our own right. Then, we can ask questions about another person's desires to make a difference. We can ask about their interests and dreams instead of presenting our needs. Together we discover an aspiration that compels action."

When we understand others' motivations, we become more competent philanthropists ourselves. We move forward knowing that the power of the U.S. Constitution is under us. That treasure of a document is fertile ground from where the citizens' seeds for community strength grow.

Fred Alvis Bleeke (pronounced Blakey) taught history, government, and economics before his twenty-five-year career in fundraising (first class of Certified Fund Raising Executives [CFRE] in 1981) and eleven years as president of a grantmaking foundation. For five years, he also taught resource development for nonprofit organizations in University College at Washington University in St. Louis.

INDEX

ABOUT MARTIN LEIFELD

Martin Leifeld has spent over forty years in senior fundraising leadership and executive roles. Lastly, as vice chancellor for university advancement at the University of Missouri-St. Louis, he led a dramatic, 375% increase in fundraising, averaging $26.3 million per year.

Martin established the website martinleifeld.com as a resource for those engaged in fundraising and leadership. The site features "Five Minutes for Fundraising," a series of fifty brief, easily consumable video presentations about various fundraising matters, primarily focusing upon the work of major gift fundraising. Martin is now releasing videos on leadership topics in addition to his ongoing development of videos for fundraisers.

Dear Reader,

Thank you so much for reading *Five Minutes for Fundraising*. I hope it further clarified and deepened your understanding of the fundraising process and will inspire and enable you to be effectively engaged as a fundraiser, whether as a volunteer or as a professional.

Your feedback is most important to me. Please take a few minutes to post an online review. Just a sentence or two would be great.

I would love to learn about your thoughts, experiences and ideas. Please email me at Martin@martinleifeld.com.

If you email me, I will send to you my latest article entitled, "Seven Foundational Success Factors for Major Gift Fundraisers." You will be encouraged by it.

Gratefully yours –

Martin Leifeld

Made in the USA
Columbia, SC
03 June 2018